An Introduction to The Cor
Blues

1932 - 1939

The Salamanca Press

An Introduction to The Cornish Concertina Blues

1932 - 1939

Collected Writings and Field Recordings

By Eric Valletort FRS

The Salamanca Press

An imprint of Libros Lavapiés

ISBN: 9798856835112

Enquiries: jpengelly2003@yahoo.co.uk

Foreword

As I stare from my study window across the arable fields of Middle Taphouse, my mind goes back to the first time I came across the vagrant musicians whose output I was to spend the next decade recording. It was at the height of the blazing summer of 1932. The sun shone, the wheat grew high and golden, and I was a young man on a quest for musicological adventure. I had my father's field-recording equipment in my knapsack and the world at my feet. Then I heard the sound of Endellion Trebetherick's concertina.

With the abandon of youth, I followed the noise to its source. Trebetherick was, as I recall, seated in the shade beneath the old water tank at Bolitho junction and was accompanied by Blind Boscarne, Reginald Lanhydrock and Roscorla "Crutches" Carluddon. I opened my notebook and listened intently as they played. Gradually the full extent of the musical incompetence before me became grotesquely apparent. It was not solely the tunelessness that I found so offensive, it was the boorish approach, the slipshod attitude towards both melody and rhythm, it was the sheer lack of consideration for the listener that immediately convinced me that I should look elsewhere for something more worthy of being committed to acetate. And so began years of painstaking and ultimately fruitless questing for some semblance of talent or finesse amongst the travelling men and women who, during the dark years between the wars, called the Cornish road their home.

Despite the lack of artistic worth or substance that my ethnomusicological excavations have, in the final analysis, uncovered, it is assuredly fair to say that a life spent in pursuit of musical diamonds-in-the-rough has had its moments of interest. Also fair, I believe, is the reputation I have gained for assiduousness and perspicacity throughout the many years of my study. (In an otherwise grudging piece, amateur musicologist The Reverend Ernest Barrington referred to me as "the doyen of researchers into this rightly neglected field."). It is for these reasons, and in the hope that future readers may gain some understanding of the hardships and frustrations of such cultural endeavours, that I have chosen to share an anthology of my writing pertaining to the years of my research. In the unlikely event that the reader should wish to hear for themselves the full extent of the musical ineptitude I was so regularly exposed to, the field recordings under discussion are also available using the attached digital linkage.

It is customary in an introduction such as this to make acknowledgement of support and assistance received. However, as I, through no fault of my own, have consistently been the victim of ignorance and ridicule from my peers, and have been cruelly shunned by the folk music establishment throughout my professional career, I will refrain from so doing.

A Short History

In order to introduce readers to the musical milieu under discussion, I am here reproducing an article originally written for (and rejected by) the English Folk Dance and Song Society quarterly journal in 1939.

"It often comes as a surprise to students of the indigenous music of these islands that a whole sub-sub-genre was able to grow up, flourish, and within a few a few short years wither and die without its coming to the attention of scholars and the wider public. This sub-sub-genre was variously known as Cornish Vagrant, Cornish Hobo or, more commonly (but less accurately), The Cornish Concertina Blues.

The players of this music were, almost without exception, impoverished and ill-educated. Many had been forced to leave home due to penury, and all had adopted an itinerant lifestyle that entailed almost constant movement in the quest for employment and/or betterment in circumstances. While many of the miles travelled by these men and women were covered on foot, many more were covered by the expedient of stowing away in dark corners of railway trucks and wagons. Goods trains were, these wayfarers discovered, a rapid, cheap and reasonably convenient means of moving around the Duchy. The illegality and potential dangers inherent in this mode of transport were widely ignored and were generally regarded as being of secondary importance when compared to the advantages of speed and cost. Indeed, amongst these travelling men and women, a culture of celebration tended to surround the act of freight-hopping, and the author has on many occasions been witness to tramps talking breathlessly of the excitement and even the romance of ticketless train travel.

Employment opportunities awaiting these voyagers at the end of the line were usually agricultural and always short term. Typically, the migrant workforce would follow harvests and, between seasons, would turn their hands to any toil that would pay. It should also be pointed out, lest one paint too wholesome a view of the individuals under discussion, that criminal activity and recidivism were rife within this community. Common theft and burglary were staple activities, while alongside this there were numerous examples of more imaginative, and violent, felony. (This, I might add, was not without benefit to the ethnomusicologist - a number of what are regarded as my most significant field recordings took place in the exercise yard at Liskeard Gaol.)

As the 1930s dawned, and the subsequent, economically bleak, months and years rolled by, these tramps became ever more numerous, and it became common for them to establish semi-permanent camps close to worksites and suitable locations for boarding and/or dropping off freight trains. Such camps were almost always in isolated woodland, far distant from respectable society, and they rapidly became the hub of the vagabonds' cultural activity, to wit: drinking, storytelling, fighting, and, of primary interest, music making.

The earliest recorded examples of this music often feature unaccompanied singing and alcohol-induced choral chants. Quickly however, tramps who carried instruments amongst their meagre possessions also began to coalesce around the trackside campfires. The music that emerged from these alliances was unlike parallel developments in English folk and popular music of the time, and in some ways has more in common with the Blues, Cajun and early Country traditions that were flourishing in North America concurrently (the arrival in Cornwall of North Carolinian harmonicist Wheal Honey Brown proving particularly significant in this respect). Choice of instrumentation was influenced predominantly by factors of price, availability (including the ease with which an instrument might be filched from an unsuspecting vendor) and portability. Consequently, the instruments that featured most regularly in recorded sides were the harmonica, versions of a ukulele, and the instrument that has become synonymous with this music: the concertina. For a brief period during the 1930s, mass-produced squeezeboxes were enormously popular amongst tramps due to their small size, durable nature, their volume and, of secondary importance, their musical versatility. (The concertina's effectiveness as a weighty and sharp-edged missile may well have been a further factor in its popularity - many a tramp carried a semi-hexagonal scar on his forehead). Homemade instruments such as pan lids, string basses of various types, spoons and tin cans also make regular appearances within archived examples of this music. Given the context of the recordings (usually late at night, with a large inebriated group sitting around a fire), the inclusion of these instruments is perhaps inevitable, but, in my opinion at least, can only be regarded as profoundly regrettable.

I began recording the men and women of the Cornish road in the summer of 1932 whilst on long vacation from St Albans. My father, the eminent musicologist Sir Arthur Valletort, had recently returned from a field trip to collect ploughmen's choral music from the Cambourne region. On this trip he had by chance come across a group of vagabonds playing *Tregonna Steeple* in the corner of a field as they waited for a train. Upon enquiring about their music, my father was told of the location of some of the larger camps and then told in no uncertain terms to "bugger off". A few weeks later, furnished with this information, and carrying my father's precious Marconi, I set off to investigate this new and potentially intriguing musical genre. After several fruitless and somewhat unpleasant encounters with men and women of the road, I at last came upon Two Waters' Foot, the largest of all the trackside camps. Following my father's advice always to offer strong alcohol when approaching non-classical musicians, I passed a bottle of whisky around and had soon secured permission to make a recording. What I captured that night yielded little of real quality, with most songs being marred by Slim Tregantle's ill-judged saucepan playing, but almost at once I became aware that here I had stumbled upon a plentiful seam of primitive music played by men and women (almost without exception unskilled, uneducated, rather brutal yet childishly naïve) who would surely be willing subjects for my research and who would, as my reputation grew, surely be profoundly grateful for my interest in their work.

Many such nights were to follow. Sadly, the gratitude never materialised and the music never really improved. However, not one to be defeated by obstacles placed in my path, I long ago resolved that the study of these somewhat unwholesome characters and their amateurish output would have to suffice while I continued my search for something more worthy of my ethnomusicological expertise."

The Recordings and Notes Thereon

Over the years, I have collected some six hundred hours of field recordings from locations as varied as the interior of goods wagons, the nave of abandoned churches and the shadowy depths of sundry railway buildings, as well as from the woodland camps and prisons that were the most common meeting points for vagrant musicians of the day. This material varies in quality from unlistenable to the merely incompetent. From this collection of time-withered wax, I have selected pieces that I feel have at least some general interest, or that are representative of particular elements of the genre under examination.

In order that the reader may have a full understanding of the context of these selected recordings, I have added as much factual information about personnel, location and instrumentation as possible alongside my narrative notes for each song. Upon rereading these notes, it seems apparent that the focus of my writing has consistently been drawn more towards a discussion of the people and places I encountered on my field recording expeditions than towards a more forensic examination of the music captured along the way. Given the quality of the latter, this is perhaps not altogether surprising.

(A complete track listing and digital playlist is available in Appendix A)

Vale of Plenty

Date recorded: August 24th, 1935

Performers: Rosecraddock, Jago “Red Eye”; Trelissick, Bob “Washboard”; Warleggan, Burraton; Porkellis, “Blue” Bob; Trebetherick, Endellion; Gunwalloe, Arthur “One Arm; Connoc, Bo; Treviscoe, Little; Chilsworthy, Sonny Boy; Unidentified, multiple.

Recordist: Valletort, Eric A.

Instruments: Gut string guitar, ukulele, bass ukulele, concertina, bass concertina, concertina (damaged), one row diatonic accordion, harmonica (high F), harmonica (low F); string bass (metal bucket body).

Setting: Fore Street Camp, Trenewan Junction.

Tape number: EAV1754

Archive ID: on.soundcloud.com/foAgX

Technical note: Passing railway traffic, disc distortion.

Rights: Trad. arr Valletort

Notes on the session:

The branch line between Trenewan and St Blazey was popular with the travelling men and women of 1930s Cornwall due in part to its geographical convenience, and in part due to the frequency of the goods trains that traversed its length. Because of this popularity, a number of large camps were established in the woodland alongside the permanent way, usually at points where trains were known to slow down or stop to take on coal or water. The largest of these camps was at Trenewan Junction.

This camp, commonly known as Fore Street (for reasons that are not clear) became quite familiar to me over the years, as, along with Two Waters' Foot, it was a place where one could be almost guaranteed to encounter vagrant musicians in their natural environment. At the centre of the camp was a large fire, kept permanently alight, over which hung a blackened iron pot. At night, the flames from this fire would reach so high that the leaves and branches in the canopy of the surrounding trees were perpetually singed. Around the camp were placed logs and stones for seating, along with a number of shelters shoddily put together from discarded or stolen pieces of railway material. A single tarpaulin, taken presumably from a goods wagon, was stretched between trees at one end of the clearing to provide protection from the elements. Being at the junction between the main and branch lines, the camp was bordered by the tracks on three sides; consequently, the sound of passing trains was (particularly for one with hearing as sensitive and finely attuned as my own) both tiresomely frequent and infernally loud.

Similarly, the music produced around that huge fire was often described by me in my notes as being possessed of a diabolical quality. On the night of the recording here presented, for example, numerous songs were interrupted by fights breaking out between the various players, and an atmosphere of simmering resentment permeated the entire gathering. As usual, the inherent mutual distrust and dislike of one another felt by harmonica and concertina players was at the root of the ill feeling - this reached its peak when Little Treviscoe took exception to Burraton Warleggan's risible attempts at syncopation and launched the latter's squeezebox into the middle distance (where it landed with a brief but powerful Diminished B flat chord).

My notes confirm that the ensemble's overall quality was not adversely affected by the loss of Warleggan's contribution, though it would be fair to conjecture that Little Treviscoe's embouchure (never his strong point) was somewhat hampered by the thick lip and broken front tooth he subsequently sustained in retribution.

As is so often the case with field recordings undertaken in circumstances such as those described, the sound quality of this piece is, through no fault of my own, middling to poor.

Trevithick

Date recorded: August 29th, 1939

Performers: Johnson, Arwenack; Gunwalloe, Arthur "One Arm"; Carluddon, Crutches; Boswell, Ernest "Big"; Luckett, Jack (Slow); St John, Mabyn; Boscarne, Blind; Tregonhawke, Archibald; Unidentified, multiple.

Recordist: Valletort, Eric A.

Instruments: Concertina, bass concertina, ukulele, string bass, harmonica, 2 stringed guitar, unspecified zither.

Setting: Dry goods wagon, northbound, Fowey branch.

Tape number: EAV1874

Track number: 9

Archive ID: on.soundcloud.com/vMqKZ

Technical note: Ambient sound. Disc distortion.

Notes on the session:

It is perhaps not surprising, given the nature of Cornish vagrant musicians' lifestyles, that there was a disproportionately high number of amputees and invalids to be found within their ranks. One of the early pioneers of the blues concertina, for example, the abundantly talented though sadly unrecorded Quethiock Constantine, lost both legs (in separate incidents) beneath tin wagons at the

Calstock incline before he had reached the age of sixteen. Following the second of these mishaps, both he and his squeezebox were habitually transported in the rucksack of his musical partner, saw player Darite Tremar. Other well known lower-limb amputees were Trebyan Sweetshouse - ex-soldier and sometime oil can guitarist; Rescorla "Crutches" Carluddon - second rate percussionist whose playing I always tried to avoid recording; and Little Treviscoe - Truronian harmonicist in the style of Wheal Honey Brown.

Blindness amongst travelling men and women was similarly prevalent: Endellion Trebetherick, Blind Boscarne, Sticks Rosenannon and Hugo "Patch" Marazanvose being the most prominent amongst the many partially sighted men of the road who were active in the early decades of the twentieth century. (None of whom, incidentally, demonstrated the increase in musical sensitivity and accomplishment that visual impairment is imputed to bring).

Far outnumbering the blind and the lame, however, were the legion of tramps who had lost at least one arm (almost always through reaching unsuccessfully for a fast moving wagon, almost always whilst in drink). While this injury was often terminal for a vagabond's musical career, there were several examples of men and women who contrived to adapt their playing to their reduced status. Most famous of these was Arthur One Arm Gunwalloe who played the left hand of a bass concertina while gripping the other end with a hand hook. In this he was, by the standards of the primitive musicianship under discussion, reasonably effective. Considerably less successful were his attempts to play the guitar using his hook as a plectrum. As can be heard on the recording here offered, a reading of the standard "Trevithick" (a song not, as many believe, dedicated to the inventor of the steam engine, but rather to Armand Trevithick - Mousehole trawlerman and bordello keeper), his playing is relatively inoffensive at slower speeds, but once the tempo picks up, the sound of his clumsy iron appendage scratching unrhythmically and unmusically against the body of the instrument is both cacophonous and highly distracting. In my notes from this session (recorded on board a westbound dry goods wagon somewhere between Golant and Lostwithiel) I make the observation that the other players, at the instigation of the ever-refined Mabyn St John, wasted no time in removing both Gunwalloe's guitar and his hook from him at the earliest possible opportunity.

To the relief of many, Arthur Gunwalloe left for Canada shortly after this recording took place.

Wheal Honey Blues

Date recorded: August 19th, 1937

Performers: Brown, Wheal Honey; Macarthur, Phillack; Tregillis, Seth “Wheel Nut”; Quintrell, Harold “Red”; Trebetherick, Endellion; Boswell, Ernest “Big”; Polkerris, “Blue” Bob; Tremar Darite; Carluddon, “Crutches”; Unidentified, multiple.

Recordist: Valletort, Eric A.

Instruments: Concertina, second concertina, bass concertina, one-row diatonic, tin-can ukulele, guitar, harmonica (various).

Setting: Dry goods wagon approaching St Blazey westbound.

Tape number: EAV1871

Track number: 11

Archive ID: on.soundcloud.com/AFZwA

Technical note: Ambient wagon noise, severe disc distortion.

Notes on the session:

Amongst ethnomusicologists, I am regarded as something of a liberal. This is in no small part due to the unusually permissive stance I take on the intercultural cross-pollination of musical styles. Many of my peers seek only the purest of musical forms - forms which have grown up without the influence of any external factors. Archibald Peabody, for example, famously burned ten years of painstaking research on the day that he discovered that the Pyrenean shepherd fife players he had spent his career recording had on one brief occasion been exposed to the early work of Tony Bennet. I, on the other hand see vast benefits when musicians of one culture are given the opportunity to play with, and to shape the musical ideas of, others (I do however draw the line at saxophonists, whatever their provenance).

This generosity of attitude has allowed me to appreciate the influence of Wheal Honey Brown, the harmonica player who, with his travelling partner Cow City Henry, brought the blues to the migrant camps of early twentieth century Cornwall. Born into poverty in North Carolina, Wheal Honey Brown learned the harmonica at the knee of his uncle, and by the age of 12 was making a living playing for tips outside Durham cotton mills. In common with many of his peers, Brown eventually took a freight train north in search of a better life away from the harsh realities of the southern states. In contrast, however to the vast majority who headed for Chicago or Detroit, Brown and Henry, thanks in no small part to a drunken night and a missed train, ended up in Baltimore on a cattle ship bound for Milford haven.

It is unclear how long it took the pair to gravitate towards the South West peninsula, but Brown's playing and his growing impact on Cornish Vagrant music can be heard on recordings from as early as 1932. Having conferred with those who knew him in Carolina, it is clear that Brown was considered to have been in the lowest ranks of harmonica players of the Piedmont area, if indeed he was considered at all; transplanted to Cornwall, however, the energy with which he played, and the hitherto unheard sounds he was making led quickly to his being a highly sought after contributor to campfire gatherings. His influence was considerable – firstly amongst tramp harmonica players who quickly removed half of the reeds out of their musette tuned mouth organs and did what they could to emulate Wheal Honey's sound and insouciant attitude (Luxulyan Slim being the most successful in both respects) and, perhaps more interestingly, amongst concertina players who became aware that harmonica riffs could quite accurately be replicated on a squeezebox, though crucially without access to the flattened third blue note.

This recording is one of several I made "on the fly", in this case inside a slow moving parcels wagon bound for St Blazey one late afternoon in August 1937. I had asked Brown for an example of his solo playing, but with typical contrariness, he insisted on allowing his travelling companions to take several verses before joining in. Amongst the other players are "Blue" Bob Porkellis, who perhaps went further than any other concertina player along the road towards the Delta squeezebox sound, One Arm Gunwalloe, and, completely missing the point of the twelve-bar form with his late intervention, the ever conservative Phillack Macarthur.

Cow City Henry was, incidentally, a washboard player of much repute amongst those who appreciate such things. His belief that recording would remove a piece of his soul led to his refusing to take part in this session. Any regret I may have felt at his absence soon passed.

Longrock

Date recorded: July 12th, 1937

Performers: Treviscoe, Little; Pentecost, Cyril "Hambone"; Trebetherick, Endellion; Boswell, Ernest "Big"; Connoc, Bo; Luckett, Jack; Constantine, Trevenan; Trispen, Ezra; Burlawn, Ezra; Tregorrick, Slocan; Carluddon, Crutches; Porkellis, "Blue" Bob; Trelawne, Carey (poss); Unidentified, multiple.

Recordist: Valletort, Eric A.

Instruments: Ukulele, bass ukulele, 4 string guitar, homemade zither, copper wire banjo, concertina, bass concertina, soprano concertina, one row diatonic accordion (Quebecois tuning?), harmonica (high F/low F/C).

Setting: Main camp, Two Waters' Foot.

Tape number: EAV1829

Archive ID: on.soundcloud.com/B3Xbj

Technical note: Severe disc distortion.

Rights: Trad. arr Valletort

Notes on the session:

The body that was found close to the tracks at Herodsfoot on the morning of 15th July 1938 was eventually identified as being the remains of one Carey Trelawne. As I was in the region at the time, I carried out some research into this unfortunate young man's history. The travelling men and women to whom I spoke about the case were generally in agreement as to most key details of Trelawne's life, and were voluble in their praise of his kind-heartedness and good sense. His tale is perhaps one worth telling.

Born into relative prosperity in the Lanlivery parish, Trelawne appears to have taken to the road in search of adventure rather than through necessity. This was not altogether uncommon - the lure of the open horizon has always proved enticing to the young; what was distinct, however, about Carey Trelawne is that, unlike others who would return to the comforts of home after the initial thrill of the highway had worn off, he made the vagabond's way of life his permanent existence.

Those I spoke to were unanimous in their conjecture that the reason for this decision was, unsurprisingly, the love of a woman. Carey Trelawne met Lowen Angarrack in the summer of 1936 whilst awaiting a train at Lostwithiel. Their mutual affection appears to have been more or less immediate, and the pair were from this point onwards inseparable. Witnesses spoke of the couple's joy as they travelled together - laughing in the face of hardships encountered along the way, huddling close as they rode wagons through the night, sharing their food around lonely campfires, and walking carefree at dawn the dusty, long-shadowed roads that would lead to their next adventure.

Then, somewhere near Perranuthnoe, in the spring of 1937, Carey Trelawne awoke to find that Lowen was no longer by his side. Distraught, he awaited her return. When the sun set and he was still alone, he set off into the night consumed by the need to move, consumed by the need to find her.

She had left no note, and no sign as to where she was heading or why.

For months Carey Trelawne followed what he imagined to be her trail. He revisited places they had been together, he returned to the location of their first meeting, and he passed through every junction and gathering point of the Cornish Road. At these places, he would scratch messages to his lost love into the rusted metal of water tanks and trackside signs. Each time he passed the same way again, or retrod the same path, he would check to see whether she had left a reply or any clue as to her whereabouts. Many witnesses speak of seeing him arrive at one of these transients' crossroads - they describe him hurrying towards the nearest tank and eagerly searching through the marks in the rust before moving disconsolately away and recommencing his hopeless trudge along the ballast.

It is perhaps superfluous to inform the reader that the pair were never reunited.

When Carey Trelawne's body was found, it was generally assumed that he had, in despair, decided to take his own life by throwing himself beneath a westbound goods. There is, however, some evidence for an alternative scenario. During our discussions, "Slow" Jack Luckett informed me of a little-shared rumour that, around the time of his death, the water tank at Bohetherick displayed a newly written reply to one of Trelawne's desperate messages. In a few brief words, the reply told him to travel west; she would be waiting for him at Lamorna.

Despite the dispassion required of me in order to carry out my ethnomusicological research to the highest standard, I cannot deny that I find myself somewhat comforted by the possibility that Carey Trelawne's death was a result, not of choice, but of a tragic accident whilst his heart was filled with joy at the thought of leaping aboard a screaming train and riding the midnight rails towards his lost love.

*

It is my conjecture that the recording here-presented is one that may feature Trelawne's harmonica somewhere amongst the throng of unidentified instruments and musicians who contributed to the piece. A shambolic reading of a traditional Longrock lament, it was captured at Two Waters' Foot one evening in the Summer of 1937, around the time when Carey Trelawne and Lowen Angarrack were known to have been in the area. In place of anything more appropriate, or anything less grating on the ears, it may, perhaps, stand as a small tribute both to the young man's memory and to the fierce love that drove him.

(This observation, I should point out, exemplifies exactly the type of rank sentimentality that my late father always deplored in my work.)

Bourbriac

Date recorded: April 14th, 1937

Performers: Tremar, Darite; Blackwater, Agnes; Chilsworthy, Sonny Boy; Illogan, Probus; Pendinnick, Arnold; Porkellis, "Blue" Bob; Trebetherick, Endellion; Boswell, Ernest "Big"; Connoc, Bo; Treviscoe, Little; Burlawn, Ezra; Pentecost, Cyril "Hambone"; Unidentified, multiple.

Recordist: Valletort, Eric A.

Instruments: Ukulele, bass ukulele, zither, 3 string banjo, concertina, bass concertina, unidentified concertina, one row diatonic accordion, bucket bass, harmonica (high F), unidentified.

Setting: Main camp, Satan's Chapel.

Tape number: EAV1754

Track number: 5

Archive ID: on.soundcloud.com/1A9Bi

Technical note: Ambient interference, severe disc distortion.

Rights: Trad. arr Valletort

Notes on the session:

On a steep hillside overlooking the vast sweep of the Tamar Valley, beside the single track curving away towards Kit Hill, there was once located a small encampment. This meeting place for men and women of the road was known as Satan's Chapel. Deserted for much of the year, it was used only occasionally, and almost exclusively by tramps on their way to and from agricultural labour in the fields of North East Cornwall. These transients would typically work throughout the months of early spring, moving from field to field along the Tamar's verdant banks until the arrival of warmer weather brought the season to an end. Despite being relatively well remunerated for this work, the itinerant worker of the type in question would invariably have squandered his earnings in the flesh pots of Gunnislake and Kelly Bray within a few short days of his final pay off, and would consequently be forced to return forthwith to the hardships of a penniless life spent in the open. Satan's Chapel was often the first stop on this journey.

My sometime assistant Peranzabaloe Horningtops led me to the camp one April afternoon in 1937. (I had recently made it clear to him that I was considering dispensing with his services and he was, I believe, attempting to impress me with the breadth of his geographical knowledge). Carrying my bulky equipment between us, we made our way down a narrow path towards the sound of mumbled voices and an out of tune ukulele. The scene upon our arrival comprised a few tramps slumped beside the fire clearly the worse for drink, other men bickering over a card game and, despite the magnificence of the views across the hillside, a pervading sense of melancholy and ennui.

More travellers arrived with the passing of the "up" Covent Garden, and eventually, as the sun set beyond the hills of Pensilva, some of those around the fire were persuaded to avail us of their musical talents. Never have I heard such a collection of self-pitying, morose and wantonly depressive drivel. Every tune was accompanied by a sob story about the harshness of the travelling life, and every player seemed intent on making his instrument produce the most pathetically miserable tone of which it was capable.

There is of course some debate within ethnomusicology about the ethics of an observer taking any action to affect the behaviour of his subject - the purist interpretation being that the field recordist should do nothing that would in any way alter the integrity of the performance he is aiming to capture. Generally, I hold to this view. In this case, however, I felt fully justified in having Horningtops ply the musicians with cheap alcohol until they were in a state to play something a little more uplifting. My ruse was briefly successful (making allowance for the quality of the instrumentalists present) and I was able as a consequence to capture a small selection of relatively sprightly numbers. My notes remind me that the recording here presented (a reading of the Breton roadmenders' standard Bourbriac) was the last tune played before the bottle ran dry and the ensemble returned to its gloomy self-indulgence.

Satan's Chapel now lies beneath the foundations of the Tamar View Holiday Park clubhouse.

Portwrinkle

Date recorded: July 18th, 1937

Performers: Lanhydrock, Reginald; Boswell, Ernest "Big"; Pelynt, Duloe; Burlawn, Ezra; Constantine, Trevenan; Tremar, Darite; Luckett, Slow Jack; Carluddon, Crutches; Boscarne, Blind; Porkellis, "Blue" Bob; Treviscoe, Little; Unidentified, multiple.

Recordist: Valletort, Eric A.

Instruments: Cigar box ukulele, bass ukulele, copper string guitar, homemade zither, baling wire banjo, concertina, concert concertina, soprano concertina, harmonica (low F probable), harmonica (B flat poss), one row diatonic accordion (Cajun tuning poss).

Setting: Main camp, Two Waters' Foot.

Tape number: EAV1891

Archive ID: on.soundcloud.com/JCcso

Technical note: Passing mixed traffic locomotive, ambient sound, severe disc distortion.

Notes on the session:

The untimely death of Duloe Pelynt in the late summer of 1937 remains an event shrouded in mystery. His body was found by the owner of the Lanreath Hotel, where Pelynt was an occasional and unwelcome guest. His lifeless cadaver lay on an unmade bed, a cigarette was wedged between his fingers, and a half-drunk bottle of whisky lay upended on the floor next to the battered concertina that had been Pelynt's constant companion since he had stolen it from the Delabole general store some twenty years previously.

Duloe Pelynt was, it is fair to say, always a prominent candidate to have his life cut short in its prime. From an early age he had combined his love of music and alcohol with a predilection for coveting other men's belongings, and in particular their spouses. His start in life had not been without privilege, having been born into a prominent Moorswater arsenic dynasty; his appetites and their consequences, however, soon led to his being forced to put a healthy distance between himself and a number of local husbands, and led eventually to his taking to the road in a semi-permanent capacity.

Despite the hardships attendant on such an existence, Duloe Pelynt soon found himself to be rather well-suited to the life of a free-wheeling vagabond. He did not lack for resourcefulness, was happy to spend the days beneath the sun and the nights between the stars, and he soon found that being without a home did not mean he should be without the comforts of a perfumed bed. Indeed, his ready wit and self-confident charm, combined with his insouciant patter and devil-may-care approach to life, meant that what he termed his "batting average" with the ladies only increased with his distance from home. Naturally such triumphs were immediately followed by a rapid escape on the first available freight train.

I, of course, have no inclination to delve any further into Pelynt's immoral appetites than is strictly necessary for my research. However, it would appear that his appeal to the opposite sex was based, in addition to the aforementioned factors, at least to some extent upon his concertina playing. Indeed, I have come across several reports, from credible witnesses, of ladies losing all inhibition when exposed to the sound of his vibrating reeds. As further corroboration, I myself was confronted with something of the sort one evening at The Anchor in Downderry: in the darkest corner of the room, lit by a single candle, there sat the Liskeard Lothario - cigarette between his teeth, hat pushed far back on his head, his concertina on one knee, a dark-haired beauty on the other. As he played, two further brazen females ("trollops" is the original description from my notes, but I have been warned repeatedly against the use of this word by the powers that be at Cecil Sharp House) bumped and ground across the sawdust in an appallingly suggestive manner to the erratic rhythms produced by Pelynt's roadworn squeezebox. The brief moments between tunes were filled with whisky, laughter, and caresses from his besotted admirers.

This particular evening ended (as did so many) with the arrival of a local man carrying a crowbar. Displaying what appeared to me to be practiced efficiency, Pelynt took one look at the newcomer, packed up his instrument and made his escape through the window of the gents' urinals. The fading whistle of the midnight train to Calstock was his final farewell and victory salute.

A life lived in such a way was not destined for longevity. It came as no surprise to anyone therefore that Duloe Pelynt's journey should come to an end in a cheap hotel room surrounded by his meagre possessions and the consequences of a trail of libidinous broken promises. Confusion still shrouds the exact identity of the cuckolded husband or wronged woman who administered the final blow, but in a sense he or she only hastened the fate that Pelynt's life choices had made inevitable.

The recording here-presented is an ensemble reading of the standard *Portwrinkle*, captured at Two Waters' Foot on the evening of 18th July 1937. Duloe Pelynt appears briefly in the first verse, but by the end of the tune was, according to my notes, heading towards the undergrowth with Polly "Left Leg" Trelawn.

Penhale Was Yesterday

Date recorded: May 14th, 1937

Performers: Treseder, Daubuz; Carluddon, Crutches; Horningtops, Perranzabuloe; Tregadillett, Lol; St John, Miss Mabyn; Trebetherick, Endellion; Gunwalloe, Arthur "One Arm"; Connoc, Bo; Luckett, Jack; Treviscoe, Little; Chilsworthy, Sonny Boy; Lanhydrock, Reginald; Unidentified, multiple.

Recordist: Valletort, Eric A.

Instruments: Soft string guitar, concert ukulele, bass ukulele, fence wire zither, concertina, bass concertina, soprano concertina, diatonic harmonica (brass), oil can bass, harmonica (high F), diatonic accordion (Lafayette tuning).

Setting: Temporary camp, River Lynher northern shore.

Tape number: EAV1821

Archive ID: on.soundcloud.com/XrsRc

Technical note: Ambient interference, disc distortion.

Rights: Trad. arr Valletort

Notes on the session:

Reginald "Lazy" Lanhydrock was a ubiquitous, if mediocre, player of the diatonic accordion during the period of my Cornish field recordings. He travelled widely across the railway network of the South West in the 1930s and, with his reputation for sloth, good humour and largesse, was generally held in relatively high regard around the various campfires where the recordings took place.

As a young man he had served as a deck hand on cargo ships, making regular crossings of the Atlantic. At the end of one such journey, he jumped ship in New Orleans and commenced to travel the byways of the Southern States in search of new employment and opportunities. In this endeavour he was notably unsuccessful, but, during his time in Louisiana he did contrive to fall in love with a Creole girl by the Lakes of Ponchartrain. This young lady was, according to Lanhydrock, so devastated when her young Cornish paramour decided to return to the high seas and his homeland, that she made him a present of her grandmother's accordion. Sadly, she did not teach him to play it.

On his return to Cornwall, Reginald Lanhydrock soon reverted to the vagabond lifestyle, riding the rails and doing as little actual work as he could get away with. He always carried the accordion with him and, until the end of his days, would happily regale listeners with tales of its provenance and with the few tunes he could remember.

This recording took place on a small beach just west of the Forder viaduct on the Lynher Estuary. It was typical of Lanhydrock that he could only be troubled to rouse himself to join in with the ensemble for the last ten notes of the piece.

St Hilary's Hill

Date recorded: January 15th, 1937

Performers: Tremar, Darite; Trebetherick, Endellion; Gilmartin, "Pink" Lil; Luxulyan, Slim; Portscatho, Solomon "Chips"; Gunwalloe, Arthur; Chatagnier, Bou; Pentecost, Cyril "Hambone"; Burlawn, Ezra; Lanhydrock, Reginald; Johnson, Arwenack; Unidentified, multiple.

Recordist: Valletort, Eric A.

Instruments: Harmonica (C), harmonica (Low F), one row diatonic accordion, homemade zither, concertina (treble and bass), ukulele, cigar box banjo.

Setting: Loading platform, Latchley goods shed.

Tape number: EAV1889

Track number: 8

Archive ID: on.soundcloud.com/K424i

Technical note: Some internal reverberation. Disc distortion (severe).

Rights: Trad. arr Valletort

Notes on the session:

The goods shed at Latchley was widely believed to have been haunted by the ghost of one Cecil Manaccan. For this reason, it tended not to be frequented by travelling men and women to quite the extent that was common with other railway buildings. The night of the 15th January 1937, however, was so cold that the group of vagrants whom I came across at the nearby camp known as Satan's Chapel eventually made the collective decision that four walls and a roof was on this occasion preferable to a bare hillside and an open sky, whatever the resultant risks of a visit from beyond the grave.

Once settled around a tin can fire placed beneath the buffer beams, talk turned, unsurprisingly, to the ghost who was said to make this place home. There was some dispute about the exact details of Manaccan's life, but there was general agreement that his story contained some or all of the following elements:

Born into poverty on the backstreets of Chilsworthy, Cecil Manaccan had by the age of fifteen become well-known to the local constabulary due to his predilection for breaking and entry. However, and perhaps somewhat unusually, as he approached adulthood the influence of the church (and in particular the good offices of the local Methodist preacher) brought about in this wayward young man the desire to reform. He found steady employment as a baler, moderated his cider intake and slowly gained the reputation as a relatively upright citizen.

Love, inevitably enough, brought about his downfall. Molly Lamerton was from the other side of the Tamar and was the daughter of the landlord of the Royal Inn. She and Manaccan met and fell in love one late summer as they worked the harvest's golden fields just outside Treburley. From that time on, they would meet every evening at sunset on the Horsebridge and would spend hours softly talking as they stared into the slowly moving water below. Such apparently innocent affection, however, quickly caused disquiet on both sides of the river, and when Molly Lamerton's father, a man not known for his patience or benevolence, found out that his beloved offspring was consorting with a light-fingered lout from the dark side of the valley, he let it be known that he would consider it a significant favour if any of his patrons were to take it upon themselves to break the Cornishman's legs.

And so it was that one night at closing time, a small posse of well-oiled Devonians left the Royal and made their noisy way to the bridge where the two young lovers were saying their moonlit farewells. Manaccan, recognising the danger, gave his beloved a final kiss and took to his heels. The mob immediately gave chase and followed him into the darkness of the densely wooded hillside. For mile after mile the pursuit continued - the hunters following their prey along the rocky pathways and past the abandoned mineshafts of the valley's heights. Their shouted threats towards him received nothing but laughter in reply.

At last Manaccan reached the curve beyond Latchley where the Callington branchline crosses the road at the top of the ridge. Hearing a distant train approach, he prepared to swing himself aboard as he had done many times in his youth. Confident now that he would soon be eastbound in the night, he stood at the crossing and called out to his pursuers, wishing them better luck next time. Still laughing, still certain of his escape, he looked along the moon-streaked rails. He was then flattened by a train travelling westbound that had approached almost silently from behind.

Cecil Manaccan's body was laid in the goods shed at Latchley while awaiting disposal by the authorities. Those that saw the dead man's face all agreed that it bore a look of mild surprise.

The recording here presented (a lacklustre reading of the Downderry standard *St Hilary's Hill*) was captured at the end of the evening's music making. By that stage, no one present was sufficiently sober to have paid the least attention to the phantasm in the unlikely event of its daring to brave the unholy sights and diabolical sounds that now filled its sanctuary.

Shortlanesend

Date recorded: August 29th, 1935

Performers: Johnson, Arwenack; Gunwalloe, Arthur "One Arm"; Carluddon, Crutches; Boswell, Ernest "Big"; Luckett, Jack (Slow); Boscarne, Blind; Tregonhawke, Archibald; Unidentified, multiple.

Recordist: Valletort, Eric A.

Instruments: Concertina, bass concertina, ukulele, string bass, harmonica, 2 stringed guitar, unspecified zither.

Setting: Migrant meeting point, Bohetherick Junction.

Tape number: EAV1887

Track number: 3

Archive ID: on.soundcloud.com/NFihq

Technical note: Locomotive movement, severe disc distortion.

Notes on the session:

The importance of water tanks to the development of the music under discussion should not be underestimated. Due to the fact that freight trains would regularly have to stop to take on water, these tanks became meeting places for the many men and women who were riding the rails of the Cornish peninsula at the time. A natural consequence of this was that, during the travellers' hours of waiting for the next train, instruments would be taken from filthy rucksacks and bedrolls, songs would be sung and tunes from all compass points would be shared. Thus, the water tank became the musical crossroads of the Cornish railway tramp.

The tank at the junction outside of Bohetherick was just such a location and I had been anxious to visit it for some time. I was therefore disappointed on my arrival to find only two tramps in situ. Both of these men, I quickly discovered, were more interested in trying to get to sleep in the long grass beside the tracks than in engaging in conversation with a renowned ethnomusicologist.

Fortunately, however, as night fell, a number of other men and women arrived. Each followed the traveller's custom of carving their initials and destination into the water tank's iron before sitting down to wait, and eventually, much to my relief, the music making began. Arwenack Johnson, Blind Boscarne and Crutches Carluddon were among the small, unremarkable, ensemble that finally gathered within range of my microphone. According to my notes, their faces glowed in the light of a small fire beneath the immense, star-strewn blackness of a late summer night sky. In the distance echoed the sound of wagons being shunted in the yard.

The tune here presented is the little-known dirge "Shortlanesend". The session was, as I remember, ended abruptly by the arrival of the westbound St Erth local. At its first distant whistle, instruments were hurriedly stowed away, the fire was stamped out and each man and woman hurried to the trackside in preparation for the boarding of an empty truck or wagon.

Once left alone, I wandered over to the water tank to inspect the writing upon it. Amongst the initials and uneducated scrawls, I was disappointed to find a number derogatory remarks regarding myself and my parentage scratched into the iron.

Pityme

Date recorded: August 26th, 1938

Performers: Porkellis, "Blue" Bob; McLemore, Deviock; Boswell, Ernest "Big"; Connoc, Bo; Luckett, Jack; Treviscoe, Little; Pentecost, Cyril "Hambone"; Johnson, Arwennack; Trebetherick, Endellion; Constantine, Trevenan; Carluddon, Crutches; Lanhydrock, Reginald; Unidentified, multiple.

Recordist: Valletort, Eric A.

Instruments: Ukulele, bass ukulele, 2 string guitar, oil bucket bass, milk churn banjo, concertina, bass concertina, soprano concertina, one row accordion (Cajun tuning with flattened VIIth), harmonica (high F), harmonica (C played in second position poss.).

Setting: Main camp, Two Waters' Foot.

Tape number: EAV1825

Archive ID: on.soundcloud.com/U8Sqy

Technical note: Disc distortion, locomotive movement.

Rights: Trad. arr Valletort

Notes on the session:

Deviock McLemore's name appears rarely, if ever, in written accounts of the development of concertina repertoire in the British Isles. This omission, however, in no way conveys the full extent of the atrociousness of his playing. Born in Bodinnick sometime around 1900, McLemore was given a squeezebox by a doting uncle for his sixteenth birthday. Shortly afterwards, the youngster left home - in search, so he said, of someone who might teach him to unlock the mysteries of the instrument. Unfortunately, barely a week into his quest, fate placed Albert "High Street" Tregarrick in his path.

At first too shy to approach the older man, young McLemore spent many days watching from a distance as the wizened and half-blind Tregarrick performed on the street corners and alleyways of Bodmin's southside - persuading passersby to part with their money through a mixture of pathetic pleas, implied violence and the occasional snatch of mawkish melody on his battered squeezebox. Eventually McLemore plucked up the courage to offer his services as hat-passer in return for the occasional tutorial. This arrangement was acceptable to Tregarrick, and over the period of a few summer weeks, he shared the secrets of his craft.

These secrets, it would appear, could be summed up as: play standing up, and play loud enough to burst your bellows. Regrettably, Deviock McLemore took this advice as gospel, and spent the rest of his life convinced that the appalling cacophony he was producing was in some way the continuance of a noble and timeless tradition handed down from the musical prophets of the Cornish Road.

Furthermore, and despite my pleas to the contrary, McLemore would, whenever he saw me setting up my recording apparatus, ensure that he was both adjacent to my microphone, and that he was a massively dominant presence in every tune played. When asked to moderate his honking, he would become highly agitated and his playing would become ever more bellicose. It was, as he said, what "High Street" would have wanted.

This recording of *Pityme* took place at Two Waters' Foot on the night of 26th August 1938. At the song's end, I became aware that my microphone's filament had been destroyed by McLemore's thoughtless playing. When I demanded reparation, he once again retold the tired tale of how he had developed his playing style, invoked the spirit of his musical forefathers, and threatened to knock my dentures down my throat should I ever again question his technique.

Polhawn Nights

Date recorded: August 18th, 1938

Performers: Treviscoe, Little; Bofarnel, Sweethouse; Blazey, Camelford Jack; Ruthernbridge, Harold; Tremar, Darite; Carluddon, Crutches; Gilmartin, "Pink" Lil; Portscatho, Solomon "Chips"; Gunwalloe, Arthur; Luckett, "Slow" Jack; Unidentified, multiple.

Recordist: Valletort, Eric A.

Instruments: Harmonica (C), harmonica (Low F), one row diatonic accordion, concertina (treble and bass), spoons (table), ukulele, apple box banjo, guitar.

Setting: Main room, Lanteglos Highway permanent way menders' hut.

Tape number: EAV1814

Archive ID: https://on.soundcloud.com/C181u

Technical note: Ambient interference. Disc distortion (severe).

Rights: Trad. arr Valletort

Notes on the session:

The Lanteglos Highway Hotel was neither a hotel and nor was it particularly adjacent to any recognised highway. It was in fact a large, wooden, single-roomed hut that had once served as a refuge for menders of the Great Western permanent way. It was to be found beyond the buffers of the overgrown sidings at the eastern end of the goods yard just beyond Bolitho Junction. Since abandonment by its original owners, it had for many years been used for shelter by passing men and women of the road, and over that time it had gained a reputation as a gathering place where music and illicit alcohol were to be found in abundance. Also attached to it was a certain notoriety, based mainly on the number of serious injuries that had been sustained within its walls.

My only visit to the "Hotel" took place in August 1938 after my sometime assistant Peranzabaloe Horningtops, who had on many occasions told me tales of wild Lanteglos nights, had at last acceded to my requests to be taken there. My notes from the evening remind me, amongst other things, of the overpowering smell one was met with upon entry: a mixture of smoke, sweat, homemade whisky and unwashed clothing. The noise was similarly offensive to the senses. A number of musicians were seated on wooden crates at the far end of the room attempting unsuccessfully to play a recognisable tune, while the men and women who filled the hut studiously ignored them and continued their shouted, drunken conversations. The floorboards creaked and thumped with the heavy footsteps of inebriated and arrhythmic dancers. A certain amount of fumbled canoodling was also in evidence, particularly after the arrival of a number of female vagrants who had just alighted from the late-running Truro mixed goods, however this is not a subject I wish to discuss at any length.

Ignoring the boorish throng around me, I set up my equipment and began to record. Conditions were far from ideal and I trust the listener will forgive the somewhat inferior sound quality in this selection. The evening's ensemble included, amongst others, One Arm Gunwalloe, Reginald Lanhydrock, Little Treviscoe and "Slow" Jack Luckett. The piece here included is a reading of the Torpoint two-step *Polhawn Nights.*

The attentive listener will notice a, mercifully brief, burst of spoons from Crutches Carluddon. Shortly after he began playing, he was felled by Bethany Menheniot who, it turns out, shared my distaste for percussive cutlery.

The Girl from Rilla Mill

Date recorded: July 13th, 1937

Performers: Manaccan, Archie; Portscatho, Solomon "Chips"; Gunwalloe, Arthur; Chatagnier, Bou; Pentecost, Cyril "Hambone"; Burlawn, Ezra; Lanhydrock, Reginald; Johnson, Arwenack; Unidentified, multiple.

Recordist: Valletort, Eric A.

Instruments: Harmonica, one row diatonic accordion, homemade zither, concertina (treble and bass), ukulele, cigar box banjo.

Setting: St Joseph's (C of E) graveyard, Hessenford.

Tape number: EAV1821

Track number: 7

Archive ID: on.soundcloud.com/RkEzG

Technical note: Disc distortion (severe).

Rights: Trad. arr Valletort

Notes on the session:

Archie Manaccan and Solomon "Chips" Portscatho first met outside the Lanteglos Highway Hotel in the late summer of 1934. Both men had recently been released from Liskeard Gaol, and both found themselves in a position of acute financial embarrassment. As a consequence, the pair quickly fell to discussing possible paths away from their current predicament and towards a life of comfort and ease.

Both were career criminals, and it is perhaps not surprising that their first joint endeavour involved burglary (with a specific focus on the well-heeled neighbourhoods on the outskirts of Chacewater). Their general lack of competence, however, soon led to several incidences of their being caught *in flagrante delicto*, and several narrow escapes from the clutches of the local constabulary. Recognising the precariousness of their position, the pair promptly caught a northbound china clay in search of new opportunities.

There followed a brief and spectacularly unsuccessful interval during which the two men turned their hands to sheep rustling on Bodmin Moor. Subsequently they moved on to siphoning diesel from fish lorries in Newlyn. This proved extremely unpopular amongst the owners of said lorries and it was soon time for the duo once again to relocate. While making their escape (pursued by a local impresario who had stated his intention to drown the pair in a tank of fish heads), Archie Manaccan noticed that the parcels wagon they were riding contained various items of value. Predictably enough, the pair made off with said items and attempted to sell them. Equally predictably, they lacked the foresight to remove the addresses and other identifying marks from the parcels, and were soon once more on the run.

It was at this point that the pair reluctantly took the decision to explore legal money-making avenues. Regrettably, after some abortive attempts to gain honest employment, this exploration led in a musical direction. Both men had, in their younger days, dabbled with the harmonica, and both reached the simultaneous conclusion that this humble instrument might be their ticket away from penury.

After minimal practice, the pair took to the streets of Lostwithiel. Their repertoire was negligible and their skill-level basic at best. Passersby were, by all accounts, suitably unimpressed. However, Chips Portscatho's aggressive body language and subtly threatening nature as he passed around the hat at the end of each song ensured that they did not leave empty-handed, and the pair moved on to the next town quietly satisfied with their success.

With time, and perhaps not surprisingly, Manaccan and Portscatho's performances became less about the music and more about demanding money with menaces. Arriving in a new town, they would carry out brief reconnaissance and then begin to play on the busiest corner they could find. Citizens who had come across them before would give them as wide a birth as possible, but anyone naïve enough to stray close by or, worse, evince some interest in their work would immediately be confronted by a proffered cap and by the robust suggestion that it would be in their best interests to show some financial appreciation. This operation would continue until the streets were effectively cleared.

Between performances, Manaccan and Portscatho would travel alongside the general vagabond throng, and at night would lend their talents to the fireside music-making in the camps. The pair's rebarbative nature (as well as their lack of musical consideration) meant that they were never particularly popular amongst their fellow travellers, and my notes remind me that there was widespread relief when the duo tired of the musical life and returned to full time thievery and recidivism in the late 1930s.

Manaccan and Portscatho feature on this recording of *The Girl from Rilla Mill* taken from a session at Hessenford graveyard in July 1937. At the end of the evening, as my assistant Horningtops and I were packing my equipment away, the pair approached me with their familiar menacing demands for financial reimbursement. Surprisingly, they were unswayed by my suggestion that instead of seeking monetary reward they should recognise the honour inherent in being recorded for posterity by an ethnomusicologist of my renown. So unswayed were they, in fact, that both immediately produced lengths of lead piping which they started to flourish extravagantly in the direction of my person. It was only thanks to my fleetness of foot and to the involuntary intervention of Horningtops's cranium that I escaped unscathed.

Alvina

Date recorded: February 12th, 1935

Performers: Quintrell, Harold "Red"; Trebetherick, Endellion; Boswell, Ernest "Big";, Slim. Luxulyan; Tremar Darite; Carluddon, "Crutches"; Unidentified, multiple.

Recordist: Valletort, Eric A.

Instruments: Concertina, second concertina, third concertina (poss), bass concertina, one-row diatonic, home-made zither, ukulele, fishgut banjo, harmonica (various).

Setting: Third arch from the left, Truro Station Approach viaduct.

Tape number: EAV1898

Track number: 24

Archive ID: on.soundcloud.com/WRuAX

Technical note: Ambient noise: overhead train wheels; severe disc distortion.

Notes on the session:

The arches beneath the Truro station approach were a popular meeting point for travelling men and women of the 1930s. Though dark, damp and generally foul smelling, they provided much needed shelter for those awaiting the many goods trains that would pass overhead during the night, and it was not unusual to encounter upwards of thirty souls gathered around the meagre fire that would perennially burn beneath the largest span.

My first visit to the location took place in the frozen winter of 1935. Snow fell in soft flurries throughout the city and, as Horningtops and I struggled with my equipment through the streets, we witnessed a steady stream of vagabonds heading away from the tracks towards the arches. Upon arrival, we joined the throng inside. The smell, particularly for one of my sensitivity, was indeed overpowering: a mixture damp cloth, cheap whisky, used tobacco and alcoholic exhalation; while the vision that became apparent, once accustomed to the gloom, was predictably unpleasing to the eye and is probably best left to the reader's imagination. One's ears, in the meantime, were assailed by jagged voices echoing remorselessly from the brickwork - voices that were only drowned by the truly infernal blast and thump of trains passing above.

Horningtops nudged me. I followed his pointed his finger and saw, in the middle of the fireside throng, Harold "Red" Quintrell. For once, my assistant was to be congratulated for his intervention because, as my notes remind me, the musician before me was one I had been hoping to record for many years.

Quintrell's poverty-stricken background was unremarkable enough, and his concertina playing was mediocre to workmanlike at best; his renown, however, far superseded these traits. This repute was based almost entirely on the fact that amongst his repertoire was said to be a song of quite uncommon beauty. A song that he had written for a lost love many years previously. A song called *Lady Fair of Lewannick*. A song, quite unlike the general run of dirges and stomps that accompanied these men on their travels, that was refined and well-constructed, strong in melody while delicate in form. Sir Cedric Petherwin, retired chief constable and amateur musicologist, described hearing Quintrell playing the tune as like being in the presence of "angelic flight on gossamer wings of delight"; while his erstwhile colleague Lifton Lawhitton described the composer of the song as a "genius rough-hewn from the Cornish granite whose true brilliance exploded through the timeless interweaving of saffron strands of melody".

Notwithstanding Sir Cedric's well-deserved reputation for hyperbole, and Lawhitton's confirmed status as a purveyor of rank falsehoods, I must admit that, upon recognising Quintrell's patrician profile and trademark trilby, I found myself unusually animated by the prospect of hearing him play. I set up my equipment, poised and alert. The fire burned, the shadows danced on the brickwork, and song followed song, each one drearier than the last; every last tramp with a squeezebox and a drink problem joined in and contributed to the din, while above us thundered the wheels of the night's last trains. (An example of such musical misfortune may be heard on the here-presented recording). With increasing desperation, I clung to the hope that at some point Quintrell would silence those around him and would boldly embark upon his unforgettable musical flight.

The night went on and this hope gradually faded amongst the ruins of good taste. Finally, I could take no more and, in a brief, merciful hiatus between tunes, I made the request of Quintrell that he should play *Lady of Lewannick* and that I should record it for posterity. There was a moment's silence during which he clamped me with a fearful stare. This was followed by an obscenity-laden refusal, a volley of further random insults, generalised guffawing from those around me and a hate-filled reprise of Yeolmbridge Waltz (a tiresome tune that had already featured three times in the night's performance).

Keen to demonstrate that an ethnomusicologist of my status was not to be trifled with in such a manner, I commanded Horningtops to start packing away my equipment. Before leaving the arch, I gave the assembled throng a short speech detailing my disappointment at their attitude. Predictably enough, my words were met not with meek apology but with a chorus of mumbled threats and abuse.

As we loaded my equipment at the end of an accident-filled walk to my car, Horningtops momentarily froze. Nudging my elbow, he informed me that the melody that could be heard wafting over the rooftops from the distant arches was Quintrell's masterpiece. I listened intently, bemoaning my ill-fortune to have come so close to my prize and to have had it snatched away by the capricious whims of a temperamental genius. A measure of consolation, however, was provided by the eventual realization that the much-praised *Lady of Lewannick* in fact sounded more like a nursery rhyme played by incapacitated Neanderthals than anything more ethereal.

Speak to Me of Menheniot

Date recorded: August 1st, 1935

Performers: Kilhallon; Geevor; Tremar, Darite; Polkerris, "Blue" Bob; Trebetherick, Endellion; Gilmartin, Lil; St John, Mabyn; Gunwalloe, Arthur; Amble, Chapel; Eunice, Walter "Woo Woo"; Lanhydrock, Reginald; Horningtops, Perranzabuloe; Pentecost, Cyril; Unidentified, multiple.

Recordist: Valletort, Eric A.

Instruments: Harmonica (High F), harmonica (Low F), one row diatonic accordion, homemade ukulele, concertina (treble and bass), cigar box bass, guitar.

Setting: Temporary camp, South Yard, Truro.

Tape number: EAV1818

Track number: 19

Archive ID: on.soundcloud.com/oMnkk

Technical note: Ambient sound. Disc distortion (severe).

Rights: Trad. arr Valletort

Notes on the session:

"Blue" Bob Polkerris's story could be considered as an archetype of the musical vagrant experience in depression-era Cornwall. Born into poverty in the flatlands west of Cambourne, and abandoned by his merchant seaman father at an early age, Polkerris spent his formative years doing what he could to support his mother, and what he could to learn to play the concertina that his father had left behind. He had little success with either enterprise. As he reached adolescence, young Polkerris yearned to broaden his horizons, and so one night, as his mother slept, he packed his bag and walked the stony path down to the sidings at Copper Creek.

Arriving in Truro on the last but one wagon of the eastbound mixed goods, Polkerris set off to discover whether the streets of the Cornish capital were paved with precious metal. They patently were not, and after a few weeks of trying to make a living busking on street corners by day and playing for tips in pubs by night, he began to contemplate returning to the barren poverty of his former life. Fate intervened when, one night, trying to get some sleep between the gravestones of the Cathedral yard, Polkerris heard the sound of a distant harmonica being played in a way that he had never previously encountered; being played, furthermore, in a way that spoke to all of the sadness in his soul. Hurrying to find the source of the sound, young Bob eventually came upon a behatted man of indeterminate age standing beneath a lamppost on Lemon Quay. This man was Wheal Honey Brown. Polkerris, in a break between tunes, asked if he could join in. Brown told him in no uncertain terms, and using some obscure American phraseology, to sling his hook.

Despite this unpromising beginning, the two men became long-term musical partners. Brown always insisted on keeping 75 percent of the pair's meagre takings and often appeared to consider Polkerris as little more than his personal factotum, but, in conversation, the Cornishman never displayed any bitterness about this, and always made a point of crediting Brown with helping him to discover the "almost blue" notes on the concertina that became the distinctive feature of his playing.

The current recording, which took place in the small camp beyond the Truro yards, was made after the pair had split due to musical differences and Wheal Honey Brown's fabled dipsomania. At the end of the session, Polkerris informed me, as he had on numerous previous occasions, that he would be returning home to his mother on the first westbound freight just as soon as he had earned a few more pennies. He died of malnutrition shortly afterwards.

Polkerris's story inspired me to carry out a little further research, and it is with some pleasure that I can inform the reader that, based on the accounts of those who heard both men play, it would be fair to suggest that Polkerris was, by the time of his death, a marginally more accomplished musician than his father. It should be born in mind, however, that these things are relative.

Unidentified

Date recorded: March 30th, 1935

Performers: Tregantle, Slim; Boswell, Ernest "Big"; Tremar, Darite; Rosenannon, Sticks; Trebetherick, Endellion; Gilmartin, "Pink" Lil; Marazanvose, Hugo; Portscatho, Solomon "Chips"; Gunwalloe, Arthur; Burlawn, Ezra; Lanhydrock, Reginald; Trellissick, Bob; Unidentified, multiple.

Recordist: Valletort, Eric A.

Instruments: Harmonica (C), harmonica (Low F), 5 stringed guitar, one row diatonic accordion, concertina (treble and bass), ukulele.

Setting: Platelayers hut, station approach, Truro.

Tape number: EAV1875

Archive ID: on.soundcloud.com/RRaVJ

Technical note: Ambient sounds (rolling stock and motive power). Disc distortion (severe).

Rights: Trad. arr Valletort

Notes on the session:

A small, abandoned, usually foul-smelling, platelayers' hut between the tracks at the western end of the goods yard outside Truro was the occasional meeting place for many primitive musicians of the mid to late 1930s. The building's position at the confluence of several branch and main lines meant that those who were heading to all four corners of the peninsula would oftentimes find themselves drawn towards its shelter as they awaited their next train. Despite its diminutive size, the hut could accommodate a surprising number of travellers, in part due to the general lack of squeamishness about personal space that these men and women displayed, and on most evenings there would be at least a handful of itinerant instrumentalists present.

The occasion of the recording here presented was my first visit to the location. I had been guided to it by Perranzabaloe Horningtops as part of my quest to gain as broad an experience as possible of the Cornish vagrant musical diaspora. The evening in question was storm-filled and the roof leaky. For several hours after our arrival, the hut remained deserted and I began to regret my decision to boycott the annual general meeting of the Devon and Cornwall Folk Dance and Song Society (in protest at their declining my offer to give a talk on the origin and development of South Hams clog dancing) which was at that moment taking place in Bovey Tracey.

Towards midnight, my long wait was to some extent ameliorated by the arrival of a trainload of travellers who crammed themselves into the building, lit a fire in its crumbling chimney piece and displayed no objection to my recording their output. Amongst their number were Big Boswell, Hugo Marazanvose and R.J. "Crutches" Carluddon. The improvement in my mood was short-lived, however: the various concertina players squabbled endlessly (and eventually violently), the acoustics and extraneous noise rendered what was captured even poorer in quality than usual, and my evening was finally carried beyond salvation by "Wheel Nut" Bob Trelissick's waking from his drunken stupor and attempting to add his ill-considered washboard stylings to the ensemble. This piece is, perhaps appropriately, unnamed.

The Cross at Gwinnear

Date recorded: December 31st, 1938

Performers: Brown, Wheal Honey; Treviscoe, Little; Horningtops, Perranzabaloe; Porkellis, Blue Bob; Gunwalloe, Arthur "One Arm"; Lanhydrock, Reginald; Luckett, Slow Jack; Portwrinkle, Blazey; Tregellis, Seth "Wheel Nut"; Unidentified, multiple.

Recordist: Valletort, Eric A.

Instruments: Concertina, bass concertina, soprano concertina, box ukulele, guitar, string bass, diatonic accordion, banjo, harmonica, zither, washboard (various).

Setting: Dry goods wagon, westbound (poss nr. Lanteglos Junction).

Tape number: EAV1816

Track number: 5

Archive ID: on.soundcloud.com/ZFoV1

Technical note: Ambient wagon noise. Ambient train sounds. Disc distortion (severe).

Notes on the session:

It is perhaps difficult for the layman to fully appreciate the hardships that must be endured by the ethnomusicologist as he goes about his labours. This, I would posit, is particularly so in the case of a practitioner as assiduous as myself. The events of New Year's Eve 1938 are a case in point.

My invitation to the DCFDSS festive shindig having again been lost in the post, I took the opportunity to go in search of (and, with luck, to record) the Penwithick sisters. Lowenna and Ysella Penwithick were born in Rescorla at the turn of the century. While still very young, they learned the art of sacred choral song at the feet of their father, the local clergyman and canon of St Edith's, Reverend Algernon Penwithick. Both girls were reputed to have voices of angelic quality and quite miraculous harmonic purity, and from an early age they became the main attraction at their father's otherwise rather dry services.

Despite their worthy upbringing, however, the girls were of a somewhat rebellious nature and had, by their late teens, made it clear to their parents that they had no intention of remaining in the vicarage for any longer than was strictly necessary. True to their word, they slipped away one night after vespers and were next seen on the streets of Trethurgy performing popular songs for the clientele of some of the town's less salubrious watering holes. The beauty of their voices, together with their apparent willingness to "give the punters what they wanted" ensured that they were as popular in this environment as they had been before the altar at St Edith's.

Rather unusually for siblings in my experience, Lowenna and Ysella Penwithick's relationship was a predominantly harmonious one, and they seem to have lived rather well for the next few years as itinerant choristers and occasional petty criminals. Their travels eventually took them far beyond the Tamar and they soon became strangers to both their hometown and to the roads of Cornwall. My desire to record them, fuelled by this absence, stemmed in large part from the almost complete dearth of even remotely tuneful examples of singing I had so far encountered on my ethnomusicological excursions.

My sometime assistant Perranzabaloe Horningtops was aware of this, and so when he learned that the Penwithick sisters were homeward bound to visit their ailing father, he quickly informed me of their most recent whereabouts and of the train that they were most likely to be on. And so it was that Horningtops and I joined a band of strays climbing aboard the year's last westbound goods out of St Blazey. Anxious to protect my recording equipment, I installed myself in the corner of the last but one wagon. At each stop this wagon became ever more crowded with inebriated, evil-smelling, instrument-swinging tramps who would, as soon as they saw me, demand to be recorded. None of these tramps, it should go without saying, bore any resemblance to the two angel-voiced runaways for whom I had been searching.

Eventually, as we pulled away from Devoran, I succumbed to the increasingly threatening exhortations of my fellow travellers and began to record. My notes remind me that amongst the players squeezed into the wagon were Arthur Gunwalloe, Little Treviscoe and, on second concertina, the recently released "Blue" Bob Porkellis. The sound quality and musicianship on display are of the crushingly low standard that might be expected in such a context.

Despite this, however, despite my disappointment at failing to record the Penwithick sisters, and despite my dismay at spending New Year's Eve squashed into a boneshaking wagon alongside a mass of roaring and uncouth humanity, I started to feel a slight softening in my perspective as we trundled through the night. I looked around me. I looked at the smiling, carefree faces of these roadworn men and women as they grappled with the melody and travelled without fear towards the future. Something about their naiveté touched me; something about them gave me hope, and I found myself silently wishing that they might be spared the worst of what was to come. Then Hambone Pentecost embarked upon a saw solo and all such high-minded benevolence promptly dissolved into the wagon's fetid and smoke-filled air.

According to locals, Lowenna and Ysella Penwithick stayed in Roscorla only long enough to collect their inheritance.

St Enoder's Tears

Date recorded: July 1st, 1937

Performers: Tregadillett, Lol; Carluddon, Crutches; Horningtops, Perranzabuloe Trebetherick, Endellion; Treseder, Daubuz; Gunwalloe, Arthur "One Arm"; Connoc, Bo; Luckett, Jack; Treviscoe, Little; Chilsworthy, Sonny Boy; Pensilva, Wenn; Porkellis, "Blue" Bob; Unidentified, multiple.

Recordist: Valletort, Eric A.

Instruments: 9 string guitar, concert ukulele, bass ukulele, violin (bowless); 5 string banjo, concertina, bass concertina, soprano concertina, diatonic harmonica (brass), oil can bass, harmonica (low F).

Setting: Main camp, Two Waters' Foot.

Tape number: EAV1898

Archive ID: on.soundcloud.com/Sq6dx

Technical note: Ambient interference, disc distortion.

Rights: Trad. arr Valletort

Notes on the session:

The tale of Wenn Pensilva is short but salutary. Born into stolid rural poverty in St Winnow, he displayed from an early age a propensity to abscond from his familial home at the least provocation. By the time he reached his late teens, he was living more or less permanently on the road and had soon fallen in with some of the less salubrious elements of the vagabond community. He was first incarcerated before his twentieth birthday and was thereafter rarely out of prison for more than six months at a time.

During one of his sojourns behind the high grey walls of Liskeard Gaol, he shared a cell with Little Treviscoe who taught him the rudiments of the strummed fiddle. (This method of playing was common in corrective institutions at the time and was born of necessity - violin bows were routinely confiscated by prison authorities due to the many nefarious uses they could be put to by inmates). Pensilva showed some early promise, and on his release, started to make a relatively honest living playing in pubs and on street corners. Furthermore, a chance encounter with the daughter of the Methodist minister Brother Trethian Carpalla led to Pensilva's becoming church caretaker and the musical accompanist for the preacher's lengthy sermons each Sunday. A combination of a settled income, the calming influence of a good woman and the rigid strictures of the church appeared to have brought to Wenn Pensilva's life the stability that had hitherto proved so illusive. Plans were made for he and his paramour to wed.

There are few happy endings on the road, however, and one drunken night with Mick "The Chisel" Tregorrick, one of his former associates, was enough to persuade Pensilva of the inherent tedium of his current circumstances, and of the benefits of taking part in one last job. His subsequent decent into recidivism, poverty and dipsomania was as rapid as it was inevitable.

When I recorded Pensilva, as part of a ramshackle ensemble at the end of a frustrating evening at Two Waters' Foot, he had recently been released from Liskeard following an eighteen-month term for battery and assault. He was, for the entirety of our time together, drunk, tuneless and obnoxious (although, to be fair to him, this could have been said of the vast majority of those around the campfire that night).

Wenn Pensilva died attempting to board a timber wagon whilst escaping from the police in 1938. The Reverend Carpalla's daughter and "The Chisel" were married some months later.

Ponsatooth Tuesday

Date recorded: May 14th, 1936

Performers: Porkellis, "Blue" Bob; Johnson, Arwenack; Trelissick, Bob "Washboard"; Trebetherick, Endellion; Pengurtha, Twin 1; Pengurtha, Twin 2; Gunwalloe, Arthur; Connoc, Bo; Burlawn, Ezra; Pentecost, Cyril "Hambone"; Unidentified, multiple.

Recordist: Valletort, Eric A.

Instruments: concert ukulele, bass ukulele, homemade fuse wire zither, 5 string banjo, concertina, bass concertina, unidentified concertina, one row diatonic harmonica, harmonica (high F), washboard (wood and brass construction).

Setting: Main camp, Two Waters' Foot.

Tape number: EAV1764

Archive ID: on.soundcloud.com/rW44S

Technical note: Ambient interference, disc distortion.

Rights: Trad. arr Valletort

Notes on the session:

My disapproval of the use of kitchen utensils for percussive accompaniment is well-documented. Similarly, my view on the inclusion of other household or domestic apparatus in musical ensembles might accurately be described as trenchantly condemnatory. These opinions, it should be noted, are no mere whims, but have been arrived at through years of painstaking ethnomusicological research and, in the latter case, through prolonged and involuntary exposure to the work of Bob "Washboard" Trelissick.

Born on the outskirts of Mylor Bridge in 1904, Trelissick was the son of itinerant knife-sharpeners who wandered from town to town with their young child in the basket of their bicycle. Little apart from this is known about his early life, but by the age of 20 Trelissick had already been in jail twice, had been sacked from every job he ever secured, and had, through a chance meeting with renowned rabble-rouser Lelant Angarrack, developed a passion for fiercely left-wing politics. Fired by this passion, he spent the next few years attending meetings, handing out leaflets, fomenting unrest amongst good-hearted labourers and generally being a drain on society's resources.

As with so many troublemakers, waifs, strays and outsiders, Trelissick eventually ended up joining the crowds of men and women who travelled the length and breadth of the peninsula in search of casual labour. In the empty wagons, by the tracks, beside the fires of the railside camps, Trelissick quickly identified a captive audience for his firebrand oratory and his socialistic claptrap, and he would spend hour after hour haranguing his fellow tramps on the subject of the injustices he told them they were facing. He soon found out, however, that the men and women around him were far too apathetic and disorganised ever to be roused to take any effective action in order to improve their circumstances, and would, in fact, much rather be left alone than even consider rising up against their employers or challenging their betters.

Eventually, Trelissick's continual ranting became so irksome to his fellow travellers that he was ostracised from most camps and gathering places. Anxious not to lose his audience, and realising that only by joining in with the nightly music-making could he gain readmittance, Trelissick stole a washboard from a Bodmin laundry, practised for five minutes, and told anyone who would listen that he was, from this point on, all about the rhythm. Reluctantly his colleagues allowed him to return to the campfire on the condition that he keep his playing quiet and his opinions to himself. Perhaps surprisingly, Trelissick complied with this arrangement for the most part, limiting himself to providing incompetent accompaniment on his slogan-daubed washboard, and only occasionally making a whispered call to insurrection when the opportunity arose.

The recording here presented, a reading of the traditional *Ponsanooth Tuesday*, took place at Two Waters' Foot in May 1936. As well as Trelissick, it features Arwenack Johnson, Little Treviscoe and the ever-feuding Pengurtha Twins on homemade dulcimer.

In 1937 Bob Trelissick rode a milk train to London where, two months later, he was found clubbed senseless in an alleyway behind a Camden Town meeting hall. It is unclear whether it was his political views or his washboard playing that had provoked the attack.

Muchlarnick

Date recorded: April 3rd, 1938

Performers: Brown, Wheal Honey; Boswell, Ernest "Big"; Washaway, Cubert; Lanhydrock, Reginald; Tremore Inches; Trebetherick, Endellion; Pelynt, Duloe; Burlawn, Ezra; Constantine, Quethiock; St Cleer, Isaac; Nancledra, Towedrack; Boscarne, Blind; Pendriscott, Ezra "Family Man"; Treviscoe, Little; Unidentified, multiple.

Recordist: Valletort, Eric A

Instruments: Bass concertina, concertina, soprano concertina, one row diatonic accordion, guitar, ukulele, bass ukulele, zither (box?), steel string guitar, hay wire banjo, harmonica (low F), harmonica (Liskeard tuning).

Setting: Temporary camp, Tredinnick Junction (disused).

Tape number: EAV1812

Track number: 21

Archive ID: on.soundcloud.com/9q393

Technical note: Ambient sound, disc distortion.

Notes on the session:

The branch line that reached its terminus at Muchlarnick was overgrown, rusted and used only infrequently. It was, however, a popular destination for men and women travelling towards Liskeard, due in large part to the perceived generosity of the smallholders that lived along its course. The countryside surrounding the tracks was, in addition, hilly and densely wooded, providing the further benefit of ample shelter for those whose journeying had led to the need to sleep beneath the stars.

At the time under discussion, there were no established vagabond camps in the area. However, during busy periods (such as the daffodil picking season) the travelling men and women who were transiting the region tended to congregate in a woodland clearing adjacent to the abandoned goods shed at Tredinnick junction. It was to this location that my sometime assistant Perranzabaloe Horningtops brought me on the evening of Easter Sunday 1938. As on many previous occasions, Horningtops had assured me that here I would be able to capture music of quality and finesse, and as on every single one of these previous occasions, I was to be bitterly disappointed.

Even before we had reached the camp I was able to make out the unmistakable tones of Ernest "Big" Boswell's bass squeezebox floating heavily through the trees, and upon our arrival I saw to my dismay that he was being accompanied by Little Treviscoe on harmonica and Quethiock Constantine on concertina. (The latter had only recently lost his second leg at this point, although, as my notes remind me, this had no discernible effect on his playing). As the sun went down across the valley, we were joined by other men and women emerging from the fields or from the dusty wagons of the day's single train.

The music continued, I set up my equipment, and, predictably enough, my frustration grew as the evening took its course. Sticks Rosenannon, minus three front teeth, ruined every song he played on with the high pitched whistling that emanated from his harmonica; Hambone Pentecost, either through drunkenness or sheer bloody mindedness, chose to play melodies entirely unrelated to those being attempted by the rest of the ensemble; and Ezra "Family Man" Pendriscott demonstrated his disregard for common decency on this holiest of days by intoning foul and sacrilegious lyrics over the music (until he was eventually quieted by washboard player Inches Tremore who was possessed of both a solid left hook and a surprisingly strong faith).

I was about to pack up my equipment and demand that Horningtops drive me home when I became aware of a new arrival. Seated at a distance beyond the fire was a dark-haired lady who spoke to no one and who, my notes remind me, "had shimmering raven locks and coal-black eyes alight with flames of profound sadness". In answer to my enquiries, I was informed that this lady, although an occasional visitor to the camps, was known to no one, never stayed in one place for more than a night, and appeared to be on a ceaseless search for something or someone she would never find. During the evening's last tune (here presented), she pulled a pair of castanets from her bag and began to play. At the song's end, she quietly packed away her things and disappeared into the shadows of the trees.

I have subsequently carried out considerable research into this young lady, striving with my usual painstaking assiduousness to find out her history, her provenance and her musical influences. In this endeavour I have, sadly, been wholly unsuccessful.

Tregonna Steeple

Date recorded: May 28th, 1938

Performers: Tregonetha, Tristan; Tregonetha, Tremaine; Tregonetha, Trilo; Tregonetha, Trevor; Marazanvoe, Hugo; Carluddon, Roscorla "Crutches"; Tremar, Darite; Kilhallon, Geevor; Kilhallon, Trethowel; Unidentified.

Recordist: Valletort, Eric A.

Instruments: Harmonica (C), harmonica (Low F), one row diatonic accordion, homemade ukulele, concertina (treble and bass), ukulele, copper pipe zither.

Setting: Exercise yard, Liskeard Gaol.

Tape number: EAV1865

Track number: 11

Archive ID: on.soundcloud.com/TFwRH

Technical note: Disc distortion (severe).

Rights: Trad. arr Valletort

Notes on the session:

The crowd of musicians waiting impatiently for my arrival in the corner of the exercise yard at Liskeard Gaol on the afternoon of 28th May 1938 contained many faces familiar to me from my previous fieldwork. As well as the perennially recidivist Tregonetha brothers (and their perennially slightly off-key musicianship), others present were: Hugo Marazanvose (concertina/breaking and entry), Crutches Carluddon (percussion/vagrancy) and Darite Tremar (ukulele/common assault). The ensemble was completed by Geevor and Trethowel Kilhallon - the harmonica playing, semi-feral step-children of Wheal Honey Brown (who were presumably incarcerated for the general public good).

The governor of Liskeard at the time, Sir Richard Boswithick, was an old university acquaintance of mine and was (according to his own estimation) himself an amateur folklorist of some note. This particular visit had been arranged to coincide with the end of my annual springtime expedition down the byways of East Cornwall in search of native rites and rituals; my intention being to share my findings with Sir Richard and to take the opportunity to put him right on a few of the finer points of the South West's ethnomusicology. However, as I had been rather less successful than I had hoped on my travels - my attempt to capture the sound of the Saint Germans Whitsuntide Blossom Revels, for example, had been rendered worthless by my guide's leading me to the wrong apple orchard - I found myself unable to engage Sir Richard in the level of debate I had anticipated, and so had to content myself with carrying out a recording of whatever this bedraggled and unprepossessing group of prison inmates produced if I was not to return home empty handed.

(There are of course some amongst my fellow musicologists who regard penal institutions, cut off from the outside world as they are, as being a seeding ground for folkloric musicianship of significant purity. I have never subscribed to this view, and consider that those who have chosen to transgress society's regulations should have no special musical prestige bestowed upon them.)

The piece here presented, a two-step most commonly known as *Oh Tregantle* or *Tregonna Steeple*, was the final tune played in the session. Shortly after it had finished, prison officers returned the men to their cells. Regrettably, this meant that I was unable to present the convicts with the copies of my pamphlet "Self-Betterment Through Communal Clog and Folk Dance" that I had intended as recompense for their playing.

Venterdon Belle

Date recorded: August 26th, 1935

Performers: Kilhallon, Trethowel; Kilhallon; Geevor; Tremar, Darite; Trebetherick, Endellion; Gilmartin, Lil; St John, Mabyn; Gunwalloe, Arthur; Amble, Chapel; Eunice, Walter “Woo Woo”; Lanhydrock, Reginald; Horningtops, Perranzabuloe; Unidentified, multiple.

Recordist: Valletort, Eric A.

Instruments: Harmonica (High F), harmonica (Low F), one row diatonic accordion, homemade ukulele, concertina (treble and bass), banjo, cigar box bass, guitar (penknife slide).

Setting: Dry goods wagon (interior), GWR mainline between Moorswater and Rosecraddock.

Tape number: EAV1823

Track number: 12

Archive ID: on.soundcloud.com/6Vxt1

Technical note: Ambient sound. Disc distortion (severe).

Rights: Trad. arr Valletort

Notes on the session:

It is, I believe, fair to suggest that when I began my studies in ethnomusicology I could not have foreseen that sharing the inside of a freight wagon with a large group of travelling men and women would form a part of my research. However, over the years such undertakings, though highly unpleasant and potentially illegal, did provide me with a significant quantity of recorded material to analyse. This material, while of uniformly poor quality both in terms of sound quality and in terms of the musicianship on display, had the one redeeming feature that it could at least be said to be accurately representative of Cornish sub-genre at the heart of my study.

The recording here presented took place in late August 1935. My sometime guide Perranzabaloe Horningtops had led me to a secluded spot just outside Lower Clicker where, he informed me, trains were in the habit of slowing to a walking pace due to the steepness of the line's gradient. As the day's light faded, we waited in the shelter of the trees by the tracks. The floor around us was strewn with empty cans and half-smoked cigarettes, evidence, I imagined, of those who had passed this way before us. In the strongest terms I cautioned Horningtops to ensure that my equipment was kept safe during the boarding of the train, whatever personal sacrifice on his part that this might entail.

In the distance we heard the low whistle of an oncoming train. Horningtops started mumbling details about the class of locomotive, the goods being carried and various other inconsequential facts; I left him in no doubt as to my indifference. Beneath us the ground shook as, buried within swathes of steam, the train approached. Its headlight cut knifelike through the darkness before us. Horningtops pulled me by the arm towards the tracks. Several wagons passed, each blasting gusts of dusty wind into our faces. Horningtops pointed: further down the train, a gloved hand was waving from the open door of a dry goods truck. At my guide's prompting, I started to run. I reached out for something to hold. Just as I felt I might be left behind, or worse, by the accelerating leviathan above me, the same gloved hand helped me aboard. Horningtops followed shortly after, showing scant regard, I should point out, for the safety of my equipment.

Once my eyes had become accustomed to the dim light inside the wagon, I made out several familiar faces. Reginald Lanhydrock lay sleeping in the corner, One Arm Gunwalloe was whittling a stick he held fast between his teeth, and the Kilhallon Twins were attempting to relieve the unwary of their possessions. Others sat and smoked and looked out of the open door at the passing moonlit countryside and the vast, distant sky.

The song here presented started as the train pulled out of Moorswater. It was initially led by Mabyn St John, unusual amongst travelling folk for her restraint and relatively good taste. As the train picked up speed, however, Gunwalloe joined in with his elephantine bass concertina musings, and by the time we reached St Pinnock, anyone who had even the most tenuous claim to be a musician was stridently making their contribution. My notes remind me that "raucous laughter floated through the thick air between snatches of melody, while smiles broke across the worn and weather-beaten faces of the vagabond throng as each rocked forward and back in time to the tune's vague rhythm and the wagon's juddering motion". I did little to hide my disapproval.

Horningtops and I disembarked when the train stopped for water at Rosecraddoc. Once my equipment had been safely stowed in the boot of a passing taxi, I dismissed my guide and directed the driver towards Middle Taphouse. As we drove through the darkness of the high-hedged Cornish lanes, I reflected on the journeys that my research had taken me on. Journeys that were, indeed, not what I might have imagined lay before me when, on that far off day in Saint Albans, I, as a fresh-faced youngster, ascended the stairs of the temporary staging to have bestowed upon me the honour of a Bachelor's Degree in Ethnomusicology and Regional Dance History (lower second class).

Kensa Blue

Date recorded: August 26th, 1935

Performers: Brown, Wheal Honey; Gunwalloe, Arthur "One Arm"; Tremar, Darite; Treviscoe, Little; Boswell, Ernest "Big"; Lanhydrock, Reginald; Luckett, Jack (Slow); Tregonhawke, Archibald; Unidentified, multiple.

Recordist: Valletort, Eric A.

Instruments: Concertina (3 possibly4), bass concertina, ukulele, string bass, harmonica (low F), banjo, 10 button accordion, 2 stringed guitar, unspecified zither.

Setting: Migrant camp, between St Cleer and Slaughterbridge.

Tape number: EAV1834

Track number: 6

Archive ID: on.soundcloud.com/VYsUw

Technical note: Outdoor ambience, wind, severe disc distortion.

Notes on the session:

The two men walking side by side on the road to Slaughterbridge exchanged few words as they moved slowly towards the horizon. Their boots scuffed up clouds of white dust that obscured their lower legs, and every so often one or other would kick a stone a few feet further down the road. Whether this was by accident or by design was hard to ascertain.

It was the late summer of 1935. My car stood lifeless on the verge, the several efforts I had made to restart it having met with no response. Being unsure of how to deal with this mechanical crisis, and being of a naturally curious bent, I decided, instead of remaining with my vehicle, to follow the two wanderers on their dusty journey.

For the next few miles they continued their shambling progress along the main road. Both stared silently ahead, and neither made any acknowledgement of the cars and lorries that would occasionally pass them by. Then, just before the crossroads at Trevagethan, the two men took to a narrow and overgrown path that led through fields high with corn towards a well-kept, prosperous looking farm building. The woman who opened the door in answer to their knock looked at the men with deep suspicion and then, in reply to their polite request for work, gave them an answer that left both visibly diminished.

For the rest of that blisteringly hot day, I followed the pair as they looked for employment. Time and again the scene would be replayed: at the end of a dusty trail across golden fields, they would knock upon a door and would offer their services. And time and again, I would watch their shoulders drop at the inevitable dismissal that would follow.

As the sun started to fall, the two men at last stopped to rest. Seated on an old sleeper beside the single line to St Cleer, they smoked feeble looking cigarettes and drank from filthy bottles. One of the men produced the crumbled remains of a pasty from his shirt pocket. He lifted it towards his mouth, then paused, broke it in half and shared it with the man beside him.

Their search continued into the darkness. Sometimes on the roads between farms, the men would accompany their footsteps with frail melodies played on a two stringed ukulele and a rusted concertina. Still they exchanged few words. Still they were met with hard faces and hostile words at every door upon which they knocked.

At a small trackside camp not far from where I had first come across them, the men's journey finally came to an end. Others were there, and many similar stories were told of lives of hunger and helplessness. Of the seemingly endless search for a step on the ladder. Of hopes crushed. The weight of misery filled the thick evening air, and the foreknowledge of tomorrow's struggle hung like smoke over the assembled company until at last, as the defeated voices grew too tired to talk, a degree of comfort was found in pinecone whisky and old familiar songs played to a star-filled sky in the light of a dying fire.

I set up my recording equipment.

Being of a naturally compassionate bent, I felt a not inconsiderable degree of sympathy for the plight of those around me. My notes, however, remind me that these feelings were tempered by my firm conviction that hard times and the occasionally exacting realities of modern life should be no justification for self-pity, and moreover that slapdash and inferior musicianship of the type that I had the misfortune to witness that night on the road to Slaughterbridge should under no circumstances be excused or encouraged whatever the economic conditions of those who produce it.

(At the end of the evening I dispatched my sometime assistant Peranzabloe Horningtops - who happened to be amongst the gathered throng - to go in search of petrol for my car. He was less than gracious when I suggested that I would reimburse him as soon as I received my quarterly allowance from my father.)

Delabole On My Mind

Date recorded: August 14th, 1938

Performers: Boswell, Ernest “Big”; Constantine, Trevenan; Pengurtha, Jack; Pengurtha, Tristan; Tregorrick, Slocan; Carluddon, Crutches; Porkellis, “Blue” Bob; Treviscoe, Little; Unidentified, multiple.

Recordist: Valletort, Eric A.

Instruments: Ukulele, bass ukulele, 7 string guitar, homemade zither (pick axe and fuse wire construction), baling wire banjo, concertina, bass concertina, soprano concertina, harmonica (low F), harmonica (B flat poss), one row diatonic.

Setting: Main camp, Two Waters’ Foot.

Tape number: EAV1810

Archive ID: on.soundcloud.com/2Zpc7

Technical note: Background voice interference, severe disc distortion.

Rights: Trad. arr Valletort

Notes on the session:

Of the many examples of mutual antagonism between travelling men that I witnessed during the years of my research, few could match the visceral loathing for one another displayed by Tristan and Jack Pengurtha. Technically half-brothers, they grew up in an abandoned mine-working in the Tamar Valley. Their similarly abandoned mother made a living from poaching and petty larceny, and from an early age the two boys became adept at these arts. Once fully grown, they graduated to the theft of oysters from private beds - sailing the river at night in their leaking skiff and scraping their booty from the muddy depths. For a number of years, the pair worked together in something approaching harmony. Then came the night in 1934 when, caught out by the low spring tide, the two were stranded, with their cargo of illegally harvested crustaceans, on a sandbank just outside of Cotehele. Both men swam for safety before their boat sank, and both men swore blind that the other was guilty when later questioned by the local magistrates. Each provided enough evidence to ensure their brother's conviction, and they were soon sharing a cell in Liskeard Gaol.

Fights between the two newly arrived convicts were commonplace, and soon became so violent that the Pengurthas were moved to opposite wings of the prison. Upon their release, both men swore that they would kill the other if ever they laid eyes on him again. This was unfortunate as both had decided to take up the travelling life, and it was not uncommon for the brothers to find themselves sharing a wagon or a deserted railway building as part of their rambling. Tales of their subsequent fights were many, and were almost mythological in their descriptions of the bloodlust and ferocity on display.

Another unfortunate element to this story was the fact that both men had been taught to play the home-made zither (of the type, particular to the upper reaches of the Tamar valley, constructed from discarded pick axe handles and fuse wire) by one of their fathers before he left for Australia. This meant that their arrival at any gathering signified not only the potential for extreme violence, but also the inclusion of a twin-pronged barrage of ill-conceived twanging. As my notes remind me, if there was one thing that my research canon did not require, it was the addition of two further instruments poorly played by a pair of oafish and highly volatile recidivists.

The Pengurtha brothers were said to have mellowed in later years, with at least one source suggesting that they ended their days running a tea room in Saint Columb Major. I am doubtful on this point.

From Pillaton to Polborder

Date recorded: May 14th, 1937

Performers: Carluddon, Crutches; Horningtops, Perranzabuloe; Tregadillett, Lol; St Keverne, Lowenna; Trebetherick, Endellion; Treseder, Daubuz; Gunwalloe, Arthur "One Arm"; Connoc, Bo; Luckett, Jack; Treviscoe, Little; Chilsworthy, Sonny Boy; Porkellis, "Blue" Bob; Unidentified, multiple.

Recordist: Valletort, Eric A.

Instruments: 9 string guitar, concert ukulele, bass ukulele, homemade box ukulele, fence wire zither, 5 string banjo, concertina, bass concertina, soprano concertina, diatonic harmonica (brass), oil can bass, harmonica (high F).

Setting: Main camp, Two Waters' Foot.

Tape number: EAV1834

Archive ID: on.soundcloud.com/THmtZ

Technical note: Ambient interference, disc distortion.

Rights: Trad. arr Valletort

Notes on the session:

Based as it was on the twin pillars of rank stupidity and an all-consuming lack of consideration for societal norms, the tale of Lol Tregadillett and Lowenna St Keverne is typical of the, in my view utterly tiresome, Star-Crossed Lovers narrative genre.

The pair met in early 1934 when Tregadillett was in hiding following his part in a botched attempt to hold up the Bodmin and Wensford Timber Company's payroll van at the crossroads south of Tregonetha. Discovering the swarthy young criminal secreted in an outbuilding close to her parents' smallholding, Lowenna St Keverne took it upon herself to bring him food and clean clothes, as well as her own sweet company, at every available opportunity. She tended to the wounds he had sustained during his escape, and played him soft tunes on the homemade ukulele her father had given her. Tregadillett's health began to improve, and the pair began to discuss their future together - a future of comfort, happiness and endless golden days.

One evening however, Lowenna arrived at the outbuilding to find that the door had been broken down, a window had been smashed and Lol Tregadillett had gone. Amongst the meagre possessions left strewn across the dusty floor was the fugitive's brass harmonica. Without a second's thought, Lowenna slipped the instrument into her bag and set off in search of its owner.

After several tortured months, the pair were at last reunited in the shadows of the water tower just outside South Petherwin Yard. Their joy at finding each other was tempered by the obvious precariousness of their situation, and Tregadillett left his paramour in no doubt as to the danger that accompanying him on his endless flight from the forces of law and order would entail. With tear-strewn promises, however, Lowenna made it abundantly clear that nothing would separate her from him ever again.

For the rest of that summer the pair chased hand in hand their mirage of freedom along the dusty roads and rusted rails of Cornwall. Never settling anywhere for long, and running from every suspicious sight or sound, they found comfort only in each other and in the fiery passion that they shared.

Occasionally their journey led them to the company of other travelling men and women, and in one instance their path crossed with my own. I was recording a large group at Two Waters' Foot when towards the end of the evening, two shadowy figures emerged from the darkness between the trees and joined the circle around the fire. One played a brass harmonica and the other played a homemade ukulele.

Shortly after the last song, the pair hurried away from the camp towards the tracks. It is said that they were planning to throw themselves on the mercy of the last eastbound of the night, a train that would see them beyond the Tamar by dawn, a train that, according to my assistant, only the truly desperate had ever attempted to ride. It is said that as they waited in the shadows by the tracks for this last train that would carry them towards the endless golden days of their future, Lol Tregadillett and Lowenna St Keverne held each other and cried. There is no record of either surviving.

(Both Tregadillett's harmonica and St Keverne's ukulele can be heard somewhere buried within the ramshackle ensemble sound on the recording here presented. However, due to the sheer number of players, and the poor audio quality - a result of Horningtops' habitual incompetence - it is inordinately difficult to tell which of the many slightly out of tune contributions is theirs.)

Up Polbathic

Date recorded: 12th July 1936

Performers: Lanhydrock, Reginald; Tregonhawke, Ezra "The Cardinal"; Brown, Wheal Honey; Tremar, Darite; Horningtops, Perranzabaloe; Porkellis, Blue Bob; Gunwalloe, Arthur "One Arm; Maranzavoe, "Patches"; Portwrinkle, Blazey; Pentecost, Cyril "Hambone"; Unidentified, multiple.

Recordist: Valletort, Eric A.

Instruments: Caradon tuned concertina, bass concertina, diatonic accordion, fusewire banjo, oil can (possibly), harmonica, zither, percussion (various).

Setting: Down avoiding line, Bristol Temple Meads.

Tape number: EAV1867

Track number: 4

Archive ID: on.soundcloud.com/K3yG8

Technical note: Ambient station noise, disc distortion (severe).

Notes on the session:

Quite how I came to be sharing a dry goods van with, amongst others, "Blue" Bob Porkellis, One-Arm Gunwalloe, and Ezra "The Cardinal" Tregonhawke whilst stationary on one of the middle roads at Bristol Temple Meads station remains something of a mystery to me. The episode had begun some twenty-four hours previously with my sometime assistant Perranzabaloe Horningtops leading me through the undergrowth at the edge of the marshalling yards just outside of Luxulyan. At his suggestion we were making our way towards a derelict signal box that was occasionally used for shelter by travelling men and women. As we walked, Horningtops described a night he had once spent there which involved, according to him, vagrant musicianship of quite transcendental quality (I was, of course, well used to his hyperbole by this point and so treated his description with the disdain it so patently merited).

When we arrived and found the signal box deserted, I left Horningtops in no doubt as to my profound displeasure. He, presumably in an attempt to assuage his conscience and restore my good opinion, suggested that we follow a small crowd of men and women who were at that moment making their way towards a train that was being made up on the eastbound line. As several were clearly carrying instruments amongst their meagre possessions, I assented and followed my assistant's wiry frame as he hurried across the tracks with my heavy recording equipment on his back.

We arrived at a wagon whose doors stood open. Horningtops peered into its inner darkness and beckoned me to follow him inside. Reluctantly I did so. I often congratulate myself on the personal discomfort that I have been prepared to endure in pursuit of my studies - in this case, for example, my surroundings' smell alone would have been enough to put off all but the most robust of researchers. Added to this was the incessant barrage of foul language, the billowing clouds of cheap tobacco smoke and the sight of a semi-comatose Reginald Lanhydrock spread-eagled beneath his accordion on the filth-strewn floor. I immediately informed Horningtops that this was more than even I could tolerate, and that we would not be staying. I instructed him to help me down. Before he could do so, however, the train began to move forward, and I was thrown back onto the splintered floorboards.

As we picked up speed, "Patch" Marazanvose helped me to my feet, examined my boxes of equipment and suggested that, seeing as it was unlikely that we would be stopping for the next two hours at least, this might be a good time for me to make a recording of his self-penned balladry. Incandescent with rage by this point, I informed him that I would rather throw myself into the path on an oncoming express than waste a single disk on any such buffoonery. And before they could ask, I confirmed that this also applied to anyone else on board who, through some misguided sense of their own talent, wished to have their artistic efforts committed to acetate.

I found a dark corner, sat down, held my handkerchief across my nose, and asked to be left alone. My fellow passengers acceded to my request and busied themselves with their usual uncouth entertainments. Then, somewhere east of Liskeard, Cyril "Hambone" Pentecost pulled from his bag a large can containing what he described as "Tamar Flamethrower". Having taken a lengthy draught, he then started passing the filthy container around. Eventually the can reached my end of the wagon, and the man next to me thrust it towards my face. Normally of course, I would not dream of partaking in such a base and unhygienic ritual, but on this occasion I had developed an ungodly thirst and so took a small sip.

The next thing I remember was being awakened by station announcements and a flurry of activity. Holding my head, I looked out of the wagon's open door and, to my consternation, recognised that we had come to rest beneath the glass roof of Brunel's imperious Bristol trainshed. To compound my profound discomfort, my fellow passengers, clearly still very much under the influence of the Flamethrower and quite oblivious to the stares of the well-healed commuters on the adjacent platforms, to the tenderness of my cerebellum, or to any sense of decorum, chose this as the moment to embark upon a drunken rendition of *Up Polbathic*. To my great relief, our train began to move shortly before the arrival of the local constabulary.

Horningtops later told me that he had not wished to disturb my sleep when the train slowed for Saltash, and that he had made a recording of the music performed that evening in the belief that it might turn out to be something of an historical curio. I informed him that he was profoundly wrong on both counts.

Kit Hill

Date recorded: June 17th, 1938

Performers: Porkellis, "Blue" Bob; St John, Mabyn; Rosecraddock, Jago "Red Eye"; Lanhydrock, Reginald; Trebetherick, Endellion; Kilhallon, Trethowel; Kilhallon, Geevor; Gunwalloe, Arthur "One Arm"; Connoc, Bo; Treviscoe, Little; Slim, Luxulyan; Nanstallon, Sonny Boy; Pentecost, Cyril "Hambone"; Unidentified, multiple.

Recordist: Valletort, Eric A.

Instruments: Guitar, concert ukulele, bass ukulele, concertina, bass concertina, concertina (high end), one row diatonic accordion, harmonica (high F), string bass (metal bucket body).

Setting: Temporary camp, Boscarne Junction.

Tape number: EAV1721

Archive ID: on.soundcloud.com/oQp8a

Technical note: Ambient interference, Disc distortion.

Rights: Trad. arr Valletort

Notes on the session:

A difficulty occasionally faced by ethnomusicologists occurs when the subjects of our research form an unhealthy attachment towards us based on their admiration of our work. On the evening of the 17th of June 1938 I set up my recording equipment at the temporary Boscarne Junction camp in the hope of capturing the large ensemble sound which was typical of long, drink fuelled summer evenings around the fire during the pre-war years. Although the music produced was of the usual ramshackle and amateurish variety, I was not disappointed by the session's personnel. One Arm Gunwalloe and Chapel Amble on concertina, and Luxulyan Slim and Sonny Boy Nanstallion (both trying with varying degrees of success to emulate their mentor Wheal Honey Brown) on harmonica, formed the core of the ensemble and were joined as the evening progressed by a variety of other musicians recently dropped off west bound freight trains slowing for the curve at Doddycross.

Amongst the latter was Maybyn St John whose work in the upper register of the concertina I have praised elsewhere. As usual I was impressed by the tasteful nature of her contributions, particularly when contrasted with the increasingly boorish musicianship of those around her. After one particularly delicate performance, I took the opportunity to eulogise her work and to offer her some carefully chosen words of advice. Immediately I could sense that Miss St John had taken my comments far beyond the purely professional context in which they had been offered. She moved the stump she was sitting on next to my fold-away chair and began to look at me in a way which can only be described as lascivious. Her playing became more erratic and her drinking more frequent. (The consumption, incidentally, of illegally distilled spirits at these gatherings had a universally negative effect on musical standards, but did at least make Blind Boscarne's spoons playing bearable). An already uncomfortable situation came to a head when she suggested that we should head back to my Hillman and continue the evening elsewhere. I of course replied that under no circumstances could I be a party to such a tryst, and she set about my recording equipment with a burning log.

While naturally perturbed somewhat by this turn of events, my dedication to the ethnomusicological craft remained unshaken and, with what many would consider remarkable sang-froid, I made running repairs and replaced the wax cylinders in time to record the night's last tune: *Kit Hill.* Mabyn St John's deliberately irritating, sarcasm drenched ostinato can be heard throughout.

Rose An Grouse

Date recorded: May 14th, 1937

Performers: Tremar, Darite; Illogan, Probus; Pendinnick, Arnold; Fleet, Fetter; Porkellis, “Blue” Bob; Trelissick, Bob “Washboard”; Trebetherick, Endellion; Gunwalloe, Arthur “One Arm; Connoc, Bo; Treviscoe, Little; Chilsworthy, Sonny Boy; Burlawn, Ezra; Pentecost, Cyril “Hambone”; Unidentified, multiple.

Recordist: Valletort, Eric A.

Instruments: 7 string guitar, concert ukulele, bass ukulele, zither, 5 string banjo, concertina, bass concertina, unidentified concertina, one row diatonic accordion, bucket bass, harmonica (high F), spoons (dessert).

Setting: Main camp, Two Waters’ Foot.

Tape number: EAV1765

Archive ID: on.soundcloud.com/zHgAJ

Technical note: Ambient interference, severe disc distortion.

Rights: Trad. arr Valletort

Notes on the session:

As was the case with a considerable proportion of the travelling men and women I came across during the course of my research, it was often extremely difficult to tell fact from fiction when one was subjected to the autobiographical anecdotes of Fetter "Two Blades" Fleet. Originally from London, he claimed to have been born just off the Portobello Road at the turn of the century. I have no reason to disbelieve this. That he died in Liskeard Gaol some four decades later is a matter of public record. The events of the intervening years are much harder to piece together, not least because Fleet, who loved to regale fellow travellers with tales of his own supposed derring-do, particularly around the circumstances of his arrival in Cornwall, never stuck to the same story twice.

Every version of his tale, however, had one unifying element - namely, a dark-eyed woman he met beneath a lamppost on a rainy night outside the Willesden Junction Hotel. In one retelling, this woman persuaded Fleet to join her in the burglary of a wealthy local's nearby dwelling. The enterprise was initially successful (the wealthy local's wife's jewel box being securely tucked under Fleet's arm), but went disastrously wrong when the pair were noticed by a guard dog as they made their getaway through the darkness of a back alleyway. The dog's barking attracted the attention of a policeman who gave chase along the cobbles. Realising that escape was impossible unless they split up, Fleet thrust the stolen bounty into the young woman's hands and kissed her cheek before running off in the other direction. The policeman obliged by following him. Fleet describes how he then escaped the justice that rightfully awaited him by wading across the canal, scaling the wall of the nearby railway yard and boarding a fast moving westbound dry goods wagon that whisked him away from the London smog and through the outer suburbs before eventually depositing him at a siding just outside St Columb Major.

In another version of the story, Fleet claimed that the woman had inveigled him to clean out a jeweller's display case while she distracted the fresh faced young shop assistant. At other times he would speak of how the pair had worked together to pick the pockets of prosperous-looking and easily diverted individuals on the Kilburn High Road. Once, I recall, he claimed that she had involved him in the armed robbery of a petrol station and, on the same evening, around the same camp fire, he told of how she had demanded his assistance in forcing a London Underground ticket collector, with the threat of a length of lead piping, to hand over the day's takings. Just as they always began in the same way, these tales, whatever their narrative arc, always ended with the dark-eyed girl running away into the Willesden night laden with ill-gotten gains as her paramour was forced to take to the rails, westbound, never to return.

Everyone who ever came across Fleet during the many years of his Cornish exile soon noticed that his conversation would invariably turn to this woman, her beauty and her malign influence on his life. Perhaps unsurprisingly, everyone who ever came across Fleet soon learned to do whatever they could to avoid him.

His only other topic of discussion was the magnitude of the punishment that awaited him should the local constabulary ever catch up with him and realise his true identity. Indeed, those who did witness his eventual arrest (on a quiet afternoon in 1938 at a crossroads just outside Lanlivery) all agree that in his eyes was a look not of sorrow but of fiery pride as he was led away by the constables. Witnesses also confirm that it was the name of the girl he met on a rainy night in Willesden that was on his lips as he lay dying on a steel bed in the prison infirmary a few years later.

(Incidentally, Fleet would also occasionally describe how he had developed his "West End" style of spoons playing as a result of hours of practice under the watchful eye of his maternal grandfather Albert "Clicker" Lee. As can be heard from his efforts on this recording, the suggestion that he spent any time at all practising the instrument is a falsehood easily proved.)

Arsenic Eyes

Date recorded: September 14th, 1937

Performers: Tremar, Darite; Trebetherick, Endellion; Gilmartin, “Pink” Lil; Luxulyan, Slim; Portscatho, Solomon “Chips”; Gunwalloe, Arthur; Chatagnier, Bou; Eunice, Walter “Woo Woo”;; Burlawn, Ezra; Lanhydrock, Reginald; Horningtops, Perranzabuloe; Unidentified, multiple.

Recordist: Valletort, Eric A.

Instruments: Harmonica (C), harmonica (Low F), one row diatonic accordion, homemade zither, concertina (treble and bass), ukulele, banjo, cigar box maraca.

Setting: Woodland beneath 3rd arch from the West, Merrymeet Viaduct.

Tape number: EAV1878

Archive ID: on.soundcloud.com/CrsDQ

Technical note: Ambient sound: passing Cornish Riviera (Up). Disc distortion (severe).

Rights: Trad. arr Valletort

Notes on the session:

Reginald Lanhydrock was apparently unaware that his American wanderings, and more specifically his dalliance with a Creole girl by the Lakes of Ponchartrain (an encounter discussed at some length previously), had resulted in the birth of a child. This state of happy ignorance lasted until the night in 1937 when he was accosted by a young man carrying a Cajun one-row accordion in a goods shed just outside of South Petherwin. Those present at the meeting attest to there being a clear family resemblance between the two men, a resemblance which raised suspicions that were later confirmed by an immediately recognisable shared playing style. Lanhydrock Senior, however, while not unfriendly, steadfastly refused to acknowledge paternity, and to the end of his days would declare to anyone who would listen that he had left the woman in question with nothing but happy memories and a minor infection as souvenirs of his visit.

When I heard about the arrival of this young man, who went by the name of Bou Chataignier, I was anxious to record him in case his musicianship proved to be of a higher pedigree than that of the travelling men and women I had so far encountered. In this hope I was to be disappointed - he did indeed sound just like his alleged father, with all the slipshod technique and lack of attention to detail that this implies. To make matters worse, the young man's travelling companion, one Walter "Woo Woo" Eunice, insisted on providing accompaniment on a species of maraca fashioned from handfuls of gravel encased in a cigar box. Chataignier and Eunice had, apparently, been friends since childhood and had performed together for many years on street corners in Louisiana before stowing away on a transatlantic freighter; perhaps as a result of the longevity of this partnership, my polite request that "Woo Woo" take his maracas elsewhere for the duration of the recording session was not met favourably. It was met in fact with a double-barrelled volley of insult, derision and comment about the supposed ugliness of my wife (they were unaware that I was single). To my disappointment but not surprise, several of the vagabonds present at the time (including my sometime assistant Peranzabaloe Horningtops) appeared to find the pair's spontaneous witticisms and word play endearing.

This recording took place in woodland beneath the Merrymeet viaduct. It features both alleged Lanhydrocks and a regrettable but unavoidable contribution from Eunice's cigar box. To compound my frustrations, a passing train rendered the song's last verse all but inaudible. At this point, Horningtops, displaying his customary incompetence, responded to my instructions to halt the recording by knocking over the entirety of my equipment. My notes remind me that this act of wanton ineptitude, for which I fined my assistant heavily, caused considerable damage but did at least have the mitigating effect of preventing Blind Boscarne from inflicting any further sonic vandalism with his cutlery collection.

The Chacewater Lament

Date recorded: August 26th, 1935

Performers: Honey Brown, Wheal; Lanhydrock, Reginald; Nanstallon, Sonny Boy; Trebetherick, Endellion; Boswell, Ernest "Big"; Pentecost, Cyril "Hambone"; Burlawn, Ezra; Amble, Chapel; Nancledra Towedrack; Horningtops, Unidentified, several.

Recordist: Valletort, Eric A.

Instruments: 7 string guitar, oil can guitar, ukulele, bass ukulele, zither, concertina, concert concertina, soprano concertina, bass concertina (x2), maracas (cigar box), fuse wire banjo, one row diatonic accordion (Tamar tuning).

Setting: Loading bay 2, Trelawne goods shed.

Tape number: EAV1853

Track number: 6

Archive ID: on.soundcloud.com/DQ42j

Technical note: Ambient sound, internal reverberation, severe disc distortion.

Notes on the session:

Within the ethnomusicologist community I am lauded, amongst other things, for my ability to remain calm in the face of extreme provocation. On occasion, however, even my forbearance has been stretched beyond its limit by some of the behaviour exhibited by the subjects of my work.

One such incident took place in late August 1935 at the old goods shed just outside of Trelawne. Having been guided to the location by my sometime assistant Peranzabaloe Horningtops, I set up my equipment and then proceeded to spend an enormously frustrating few hours being subjected to the incoherent groanings of the first arrivals - the Doublebois brothers with their seemingly unending catalogue of a-Capella mining disaster songs. Much to my relief (and to the relief of Horningtops who had been left in no doubt as to my displeasure with regard to the evening's progress), the arrival of the late-running Trevelmond mixed-goods brought with it an influx of familiar faces, amongst whom were Reginald Lanhydrock, Blind Boscarne, and Cyril "Hambone" Pentecost.

In short order, drink was taken, instruments were produced and I began to record. My notes remind me that the fruits of this session were of the usual uncultured and slipshod variety, with Ernest "Big" Boswell's bass concertina trampling over the melody like a rampant wildebeest, and Ezra Burlawn's cigar box maracas consistently scuppering every attempt to achieve even the semblance of a consistent tempo. However, as the evening progressed, my trained ear was able to discern just the slightest hint of something more refined amongst the general buffoonery. Walking around the circle, I noticed a young woman - whom I had not before encountered - playing (relatively) delicate melodic lines on a well shined squeezebox. Her playing and her general demeanour reminded me somewhat of a young Mabyn St John (though obviously I was hopeful that she did not share the latter's tendency towards emotional outburst and occasional uncontrollable violence). I listened intently.

The melody that emanated from the young lady's concertina was certainly pleasant, but was, however, almost entirely lost within the overall coarseness of the playing, and so at the next interval between songs I made the request that she should be allowed to play with minimal accompaniment for a few minutes.

The young woman (whose name I later learned was Praze Rose) thanked me and began to play. Her fine fingers skipped across the silver buttons of her instrument, and her face shone in the reflected firelight as she breathed soft sighs in time with the bellows. I watched entranced (and almost oblivious to her technical deficiencies) as she embarked upon *The Chacewater Lament* accompanied only by the reasonably restrained Endellion Trebetherick and "Slow" Jack Luckett.

With crushing inevitability however, this small ensemble was intruded on, first by Wheal Honey Brown (who had just woken up), by Little Treviscoe (whose admiration of Brown was such that he would replicate his every action) and then, one by one, by every other tramp with an instrument in that smoke-filled and God forsaken goods shed. The young woman, clearly used to her playing being swamped by the oafs around her, continued gamely on as ever more instruments piled into the maelstrom, but I could contain my fury no longer. The final straw came when I saw Crutches Carluddon preparing to join in with his spoons. Seizing them from his hand, I marched across the room and jammed the offending items of cutlery into the mechanism of my Marconi, bringing the recording to an abrupt, but appropriate end.

In the awkward silence that followed, I made my feelings clear to the assembled company - demanding at least a modicum of mutual respect and musical decorum, and reminding them of how lucky they were that a researcher of my calibre should have chosen them as subjects. I then instructed Horningtops to pack up my equipment, and together we made our way back to the car.

As we crossed the tracks, I turned to look back at the scene in the goods shed. Wheal Honey Brown had gone back to sleep, "Big" Boswell had embarked upon another elephantine solo, and the Doublebois brothers were bellowing their way through the chorus of The Wheal Thomas Flood. My notes also remind me that in the farthest corner, beside the glinting light of a pair mangled spoons, Praze Rose was running her fine fingers through the hair of an apparently inconsolable Crutches Carluddon.

Manachan Quay

Date recorded: April 14th, 1936

Performers: Porkellis, "Blue" Bob; St John, Miss Mabyn; Boswell, Ernest "Big"; Tregorrick, Slocan; Lanhydrock, Reginald; Treviscoe, Little; Gunwalloe, Arthur (One Arm); Boscarne, Blind; Trebetherick, Issy; Unidentified, multiple.

Recordist: Valletort, Eric A.

Instruments: Ukulele, bass ukulele, 8 string box zither, copper wire banjo, concertina, bass concertina, soprano concertina, bucket bass (steel), claps, harmonica (low F probable), harmonica (high F), one row diatonic accordion, guitar (open D tuning poss).

Setting: Main camp, Two Waters' Foot.

Tape number: EAV1823

Track number: 11

Archive ID: on.soundcloud.com/6HGFz

Technical note: Ambient railway noise, severe disc distortion.

Rights: Trad. arr Valletort

Notes on the session:

Issy Trebetherick (no relation to Endellion) left prison in the late summer of 1934 having completed a two-year term for common assault. Taking the Falmouth branch line, he immediately made his way to the outskirts of Helston where, he believed, his young bride would be awaiting him. She, however, appears to have grown restless and had long since abandoned the small cottage behind the goods shed that they used to share. Upon discovering her absence, Trebetherick, heartbroken, resolved to end his life by walking into the path of the first train that passed. It was his good fortune that, it being a Sunday, several hours ticked by before anything moved in either direction; in fact, by the time that the early morning Clearbrook Fish trundled through, Trebetherick was so drunk on the brandy he had purloined to help ease his passage into the next world that he was barely conscious, let alone possessed of the strength to raise himself and walk towards the tracks.

Some days later Trebetherick arrived at Two Waters' Foot. Previously a familiar sight at the camp and on the main line, his former acquaintances were shocked at the change that had come over him as he reintegrated himself with the travelling throng. The mild mannered, somewhat diffident character that they had once known had become withdrawn and taciturn in the extreme. He still rode the trains and followed the seasonal work with other vagrants, but he rarely spoke to his companions and wherever he went, he carried a small notebook in which he would write frantic notes whenever the mood took him. Many was the traveller who told tales of discovering him huddled in the corner of a wagon or lineside hut writing furiously in his book by the light of a single cigarette. Naturally, many were curious as to what he was writing, but Trebetherick steadfastly refused to allow anyone to read a word of what the notebook contained. Neither threat nor payment had any effect on his resolve until one night near West Taphouse, he at last confided to Mabyn St John that within the book was housed the self-penned poetry that enabled him to express his innermost torment. To her he described the painful birth of each line and the burning passion contained in every phrase. With typical decorum, Miss St John kept this information almost exclusively to herself.

When I became aware of Trebetherick's poetic endeavours, I resolved to judge their quality with a view to recording them as an artistic alternative to the vagabond community's musical offerings that were, even at this early stage, starting to become so tiresome to me. Persuading him to share his work was not easy, but was eventually achieved with the usual alcoholic and financial inducements. Sadly, but perhaps not surprisingly, Trebetherick's work turned out to be self-pitying doggerel of the very basest kind and it quickly became clear to me that not a word of it was worthy of being shared with a wider audience.

This recording, a large ensemble piece, possibly a reworking of the traditional lugger's lament *Manachan Quay*, took place at Two Waters' Foot shortly after I had appraised Trebetherick of the quality of his output. His somewhat listless clapping can be heard throughout.

East of Godolphin Cross

Date recorded: May 17th, 1937

Performers: Rosenannon "Sticks"; Rosecraddock, Jago "Red Eye"; Trelissick, Bob "Washboard"; Trebetherick, Endellion; Kilhallon, Trethowel; Kilhallon, Geevor; Gunwalloe, Arthur "One Arm); Connoc, Bo; Unidentified, multiple.

Recordist: Valletort, Eric A.

Instruments: copper string guitar, concert ukulele, bass ukulele, zither, box banjo, concertina, bass concertina, one row diatonic accordion, string bass (metal bucket body).

Setting: "Up" marshalling yard, West Bofarnel.

Tape number: EAV1752

Track number: 19

Archive ID: on.soundcloud.com/DNboE

Technical note: Ambient interference, locomotive movements (close quarters), disc distortion.

Rights: Trad. arr Valletort

Notes on the session:

On the occasion of my finally being invited to address the Autumn gathering of the Devon and Cornwall Folk Dance and Song Society, I was initially unsure as to which aspect of my research should form the main focus of my presentation. After much thought, I plumped for a detailed examination of the difficulties faced by myself in capturing material of any quality due to both the musical incompetence and wayward nature of my subjects, and to the ambient noise particular to the trackside locations of much of my fieldwork.

The example I planned to share (and have here presented) encapsulated these difficulties. It was recorded on a fine May evening in 1937. After a tiresome bus journey, my sometime assistant Perranzabaloe Horningtops led me to a shadowy corner of the West Bofarnel marshalling yard - a location that, he assured me, every night became the meeting point for tramps headed to all four corners of the peninsula. Unusually, he was not wrong in this assertion. With the arrival of each train into the yard, there came a new and motley collection of travelling men and women. As usual, several carried instruments, and as usual most had partaken of alcohol to an irresponsible degree. A fire was lit beneath the branches of an overhanging tree, pathetically meagre cigarettes were rolled, and the music making began.

Amongst those present at the meeting place that night were Slim Tregantle, who had recently been released on parole having served 18 months in Liskeard Gaol for unspecified crimes against society; Darite Tremar, utterly morose, and, according to himself, ready to throw himself under the next coal wagon following the dissolution of his relationship with "Diamond" Nelly Trezaise; and Sticks Rosenannon, who was relearning the ukulele having recently lost an arm whilst attempting to board the Kensington Milk just outside Bohetherick. (For those who were familiar with his pre-amputation playing, the idea that he should even consider his musical voyage as one worth continuing was the very definition of hope beyond expectation and, as I put it to him at the time, could only be described as an exercise in utter folly).

The piece here presented was selected to share with my illustrious audience as it exemplifies several of the many obstacles and annoyances regularly placed in my path. Typically for example, my requests with regard to choice of instrumentation were ignored, as were my pleas that Blind Boscarne should keep his flatulence out of range of my microphone. Furthermore, the tune eventually captured (usually known as *East of Godolphin Cross*) was played against the background of a fight between Bo Connoc and Wheal Honey Brown over an unpaid gambling debt, was nearly drowned out by the sound of passing motive power, and was performed by men and women who quickly lost any interest they may once have had in remembering the melody. This, as I have suggested, was entirely characteristic of the conditions under which I carried out my research.

With my usual diligence, I prepared my lecture complete with slides, printed handouts and audio recordings, and made my way to Bovey Tracy. I took a last sip of sherry and readied myself to stand before my peers. To my intense annoyance, however, I was, in the end, able to share but a small fraction of my research because The Reverend Ernest Barrington's repetitive ramblings on the subject of South Hams Morris overran to such an extent that as I approached the lectern, a large proportion of the assembled guests rose to leave. The church hall caretaker took this as a sign to start locking up the building, and would brook no argument as he rattled his keys aggressively above the sound of my voice.

My subsequent letter of complaint to the DCFDSS committee was treated with the same disdain they habitually reserved for my occasional requests for petrol money.

Roll Me Stithians

Date recorded: August 14th, 1938

Performers: Boswell, Ernest "Big"; Constantine, Trevenan; Tregorrick, Slocan; Carluddon, Crutches; Porkellis, "Blue" Bob; Treviscoe, Little; Unidentified, multiple.

Recordist: Valletort, Eric A.

Instruments: Ukulele, bass ukulele, 7 string guitar, homemade zither, baling wire banjo, concertina, bass concertina, soprano concertina, harmonica (low F), harmonica (B flat poss), one row diatonic.

Setting: Main camp, Two Waters' Foot

Tape number: EAV1809

Track number: 6

Archive ID: on.soundcloud.com/Ymhsw

Technical note: Background voice interference, severe disc distortion.

Rights: Trad. arr Valletort

Notes on the session:

The presence of children amongst the travelling men and women of depression-era Cornwall was relatively uncommon. Most vagabonds were unmarried and were accustomed to forming only the most fleeting of attachments; any incidental offspring pertaining to these attachments had, furthermore, generally been long since abandoned. Young Crowlas Warleggan was the exception to this rule, and his tale is perhaps one worth telling.

Born in Hayle in the late 1920s, Crowlas Warleggan lived a settled early life with his father, a joiner, and his mother, an occasional net-mender. When, however, his father lost his job, and tuberculosis took his mother shortly before his seventh birthday, Warleggan's carefree days were at end. His father tried for many months to find new work without success, before eventually deciding that he and the child should cast their fortunes to the wind. With their few possessions bundled together and tied with a ribbon from the dear departed's hair, father and son headed off into a stormy night and caught the last empty wagon out of the sidings at Copper Creek.

Their journey, once started, progressed in slow and comfortless stages: a parcels van to Nancledra, a milk wagon to Carharrack, an open clay to St Blazey. To cheer themselves as they waited in the shadows, the pair would talk of happier days and of their dream of walking the light-strewn streets of London. At last they reached Menheniot, a short stretch from the bridge across the Tamar and the gateway to their new life.

Accounts differ as to the exact details of what happened on that summer night in 1936, but what is certain is that Crowlas Warleggan and his father never made it across the Tamar and were at some point thrown from the train they were trying to board. Also certain is that when he regained consciousness Warleggan was alone. He would never see his father again.

The boy was removed by the authorities first to Liskeard hospital and then to the local Barnardo's home where he would spend the next five years. He was by all accounts a docile child, but four grey walls could not hold him, and eventually his escape attempts were so frequent and his absences so prolonged that the staff gave up looking for him.

Once free of the institution, Crowlas Warleggan would invariably make for the main line. He would tell those he came across that he was on his way to meet his father, who was always one station further down the track. The boy's lonely figure scrambling along the ballast towards the horizon became a common sight, as did the pitiful view of him building his fire alone by the tracks at the end of each weary day.

Despite the hand that fate had dealt him, however, young Crowlas was possessed of a resilient soul. He spoke little, but appeared to take everything in; he walked slowly, but travelled many miles. He quickly learned the ways of the vagabond and became adept at evading the clutches of the authorities and the various unsavoury characters who meant him no good. (In this he was helped by the good offices of "Pink" Lil Gilmartin and Nancy Blackwater who took him under their wing and, when necessary, employed their not inconsiderable knife-wielding abilities in his defence.) As he grew, he became stronger and joined the ranks of those travelling to find work. Wherever he went, however, whether his luck had been good or ill, it would not be long before he would make his way back to the place where his childhood had ended, and not long before he would once more be seen scouring the countryside around Menheniot.

It always struck me that Crowlas Warleggan was fully aware, even from the earliest times, that his father was not going to be found just around the next bend in the track. Despite this, he seemed to know that his search was not in vain. Indeed, of all the men and women I came across on the Cornish road, Warleggan always appeared one of the most content with his lot. He lived a long life, and could still be seen wandering the tracks many years after they had been abandoned by his former travelling companions. The last time I saw him was one evening at Saint Germans. I was waiting for the London train; he was reading a book by the light of a cigar. We nodded a wordless acknowledgement.

According to my notes, a ten-year-old Warleggan was present at the here-presented recording of *Roll Me Stithians.* He played no active part in the music-making as I recall, but he did perform the invaluable service of accidentally sitting on Trevenan Constantine's homemade dulcimer halfway through the second verse.

The Dark Side of the Valley

Date recorded: July 29th, 1935

Performers: Brown, Wheal Honey; Boswell, Ernest "Big"; Washaway, Cubert; Lanhydrock, Reginald; Nanstallon, Sonny Boy; Trebetherick, Endellion; Pelynt, Duloe; Nancledra, Towedrack; Unidentified, multiple.

Recordist: Valletort, Eric A (with minimal assistance from Miss E Hatherleigh)

Instruments: concertina, bass concertina, soprano concertina, oil can guitar, ukulele, bass ukulele, box zither, harmonica (high F), one row diatonic accordion (Caradon tuning).

Setting: Former ticket office, down platform, Higher Tremacoombe Station (disused).

Tape number: EAV1842

Track number: 15

Archive ID: on.soundcloud.com/RXvNH

Technical note: Ambient sound (internal), severe disc distortion.

Notes on the session:

Despite its renown as a meeting point for migrant musicians from the four corners of Cornwall, the disused station at

Higher Tremacoombe was a place I only ever visited infrequently. This was due in large part to its insalubrious reputation and to a humiliating incident that had befallen me on my first visit to the location. (I have no intention of recounting the details of this unfortunate event - which involved a rusty pickaxe and Ezra "The Cardinal" Rosecraddoc - and will limit myself to the affirmation that it was of a sufficiently serious nature to warrant an, entirely unsatisfactory, investigation by the local constabulary.)

In the summer of 1935, however, the following circumstances conspired to compel me to make a further foray along the dark woodland path that led to the old platforms: I had, as an act of generosity, agreed to take on a young student as an assistant over the long vacation; this student, a niece of amateur song-collector Sir William Hatherleigh, declared herself fascinated by the harmonica playing of Wheal Honey Brown whose work she had become familiar with through my seminal Two Waters' Foot recordings; Brown had recently been released from Liskeard Gaol and was at the time rumoured to be reacquainting himself with the pleasures of freedom in the Tremarcoombe area. Young Miss Hatherleigh begged that we should locate Brown and further capture his stylings. As her work over the summer had been not unsatisfactory, and as I was aware of her uncle's influence within the DCFDSS, I agreed to the expedition despite my previously stated reservations.

Higher Tremacoombe Station, when we arrived, was everything I had remembered and more. Weeds climbed the external walls, rusty signage creaked in the wind, and nothing but a few cracked tiles remained on the bedraggled rooftops. A single siding, rusted and overgrown, ran alongside one of the platforms before eventually being swallowed by the foliage. We heard music. Looking through the smashed windows of the former ticket hall, we saw an unprepossessing crowd seated around an oil drum fire – many had instruments, and amongst their number, asleep in the corner, was Wheal Honey Brown. Miss Hatherleigh gasped.

Once inside, and once accustomed to the dimness of the light and the foulness of the smell, we set up our equipment. My companion's presence caused something of a stir, and several scuffles broke out between those competing for her attention; I of course shooed these suitors away and left them in no doubt of the dire consequences of any inappropriate advances. Disappointingly, Miss Hatherleigh appeared to find their behaviour amusing.

Eventually, Wheal Honey Brown awoke and joined in the already overcrowded ensemble. His playing was of the usual slipshod and lackadaisical standard I had come to expect of him, but my companion appeared unaccountably impressed. She fixed her gaze on his sweating and writhing figure throughout, and let out small sighs of appreciation every time he gasped for air or wailed a particularly piercing note. She appeared entirely oblivious to the paucity of his skill and to the thoughtless brutality of his playing. "Isn't he divine?" she whispered to me at one point. "No," I replied.

At the end of the music-making, Miss Hatherleigh went to speak to Brown. A few minutes later she informed me that she would not be requiring a lift back to Middle Taphouse as she had been invited to continue the evening elsewhere by the errant mouth organist.

I of course raised the strongest possible objections to this arrangement, and we argued at some length before parting on the most uncivil terms. I travelled home alone and heard nothing from my former assistant until that September's issue of the DCFDSS journal, an issue that contained an article written by her entitled: "The Myopia of Conservatism - A Summer Spent with the Dinosaur of Ethnomusicology". My subsequent letter of complaint to her uncle received the briefest and most unsatisfactory of replies.

Several years after this recording took place, Miss Hatherleigh became (second-rate musicologist) The Reverend Ernest Barrington's secretary, and shortly afterwards his third wife. I did not send flowers.

St Macra's Moon

Date recorded: August 31st, 1935

Performers: Downderry, Narkurs; Tregantle, Slim; Rosenannon, Sticks; Trebetherick, Endellion; Gilmartin, "Pink" Lil; Portscatho, Solomon "Chips"; Chatagnier, Bou; Gunwalloe, Arthur "One Arm"; Lanhydrock, Reginald; Johnson, Arwenack; Amble, Chapel; Unidentified, multiple.

Recordist: Valletort, Eric A.

Instruments: Concertina (treble and bass), harmonica (C), harmonica (Low F), guitar, one row diatonic accordion, ukulele.

Setting: Main water tower, Bolitho Junction.

Tape number: EAV1821

Track number: 8

Archive ID: on.soundcloud.com/u1BSj

Technical note: Disc distortion (severe), background interference.

Notes on the session:

For several weeks during the warm summer of 1935, I travelled with Endellion Trebetherick and Arthur "One Arm" Gunwalloe. Trebetherick, the blind, left-handed guitarist, relied on Gunwalloe as his guide, and the pair were rarely separated. This did not mean that the two men had anything that could be described as an even remotely amiable relationship. Indeed, there were several occasions during my time with them when their constant bickering culminated in actual physical violence. (It should, however, be pointed out that, due to each man's specific disability, neither was particularly effective as a pugilist and few blows of any significance were ever landed.)

The current recording took place after the duo had spent a night playing on a street corner in Quethiock. During this performance, Gunwalloe confirmed the long and widely held suspicion that he kept for himself the vast majority of the duo's meagre takings. Towards dawn, on our way out of town, the three of us came across a large group of travelling men waiting at the water tank outside Bolitho junction. Thankful to be freed from my erstwhile companions' graceless carping, I set up my equipment to record the dying embers of the night's music making. Gunwalloe and Trebetherick seemed likewise relieved at a change in company and quickly joined in with the primitive ensemble.

The tune here presented is generally referred to as *St Macra's Moon* and was the last to be played before the arrival of the late-running Callington mixed goods broke up the gathering. As I watched them approach the train in the misty morning light, I noted with some surprise the tenderness and care with which Trebetherick and Gunwalloe helped each other to board the slowly moving wagon before them.

Trematon Yard

Date recorded: July 24th, 1937

Performers: Nanstallon, Sonny Boy; Trebetherick, Endellion; Coppa, Bos; Boswell, Ernest “Big”; Pelynt, Duloe; Burlawn, Ezra; Amble, Chapel; Tremar, Darite; Horningtops, Perranzabaloe; Carluddon, “Crutches”; Lanhydrock, St Cleer, Isaac; Treviscoe, Little; Unidentified, multiple.

Recordist: Valletort, Eric A.

Instruments: Copper string guitar, box ukulele, bass ukulele, homemade zither, fencing wire banjo, concertina, concert concertina, soprano concertina, broken concertina, harmonica (high F poss), one row diatonic accordion.

Setting: Main shed, roundhouse No 1, Trevallas.

Tape number: EAV1851

Track number: 4

Archive ID: on.soundcloud.com/QAAfE

Technical note: Passing pannier tank locomotive, roundhouse ambient sound, severe disc distortion.

Notes on the session:

When I first encountered Isaac St Cleer, he was standing in the entrance of the Trevellas Roundhouse looking out at the streams of rainwater flowing between the tracks. He was among a number of travelling men and women who had sought shelter in the cavernous shed when their journey along the Cornish main line had been interrupted by a summer storm of quite biblical intensity. Having heard something of St Cleer's history and his renown for being amongst the more intelligent tramps currently active, I decided to engage him in conversation while we sat out the torment.

He was not unfriendly and not inarticulate. When asked, he told me of his youth in Menheniot and his early apprenticeships in arable farming, courtesy of his father, and in melodeon playing, courtesy of his mother. It seemed, in fact, that St Cleer's early life had prepared him well for a wholesome agricultural existence leavened by occasional merrymaking with the local Morris side at weekends and on public holidays. Strangely, however, such a life was apparently insufficient for him and on the eve of his twenty-first birthday he said goodbye to his parents and, promising to return when his first novel had been written, wedged himself between daffodil crates on the back of a truck bound for Covent Garden.

London was, initially at least, everything that Isaac had dreamed of. He found work as a kitchen porter and an attic room to rent in Old Compton Street. In his spare time he visited galleries and bookshops, and every day he found new wonders to admire. At night, he would sit at the small wooden table in the corner of his room and, by the light of a single candle, would write of his adventures.

St Cleer's life improved still further when, on a cold winter's afternoon, he came across a young woman sketching the view from Waterloo Bridge. Ever one to seek out company, he engaged her in conversation and, when she intimated that her work was done for the day, invited her to the nearest tearoom. He quickly found out that his new acquaintance had, like him, come to London with artistic hopes and was currently working as a barmaid in a Soho hostelry in order to pay for the life drawing classes she took on her evenings off. Their conversation continued deep into the evening, and within days the pair were a common sight walking arm in arm along the Embankment or sharing a bench in St James's park - she with her sketchbook, he with his tattered notepad and ink stained hands. And now, when he returned to his attic at the end of each day, the words written onto Isaac's candlelit page were no longer of monuments or the city's great sights, but of the all-conquering power of love.

Isaac St Cleer never knew why the young woman left him. Her note said only that they should no longer see each other and that he should under no circumstances try to contact her. When, despite this warning, he knocked on the door of her room above the pub, her tearful voice gave no answers to his questions and begged repeatedly that he should leave. Eventually Isaac did as she had asked. Having done so, he spent the rest of the day, and all of the night, staggering from one drinking den to another before eventually coming to rest in a neon-lit puddle outside the Berwick Street police station. The following day, he did much the same.

Soon he had lost both job and lodgings and was forced to join those who slept beneath the Charing Cross arches. He kept his squeezebox close by and, during the day, played it for shoppers on Greek Street. Unsurprisingly perhaps, this barely earned him enough to eat, and eventually he made the decision to retrace his steps to Cornwall. Before leaving, he knocked one more time on the young woman's door. There was no answer.

Unable to face the shame of returning home with none of the literary triumph he had once spoken so confidently of achieving, St Cleer remained a man of the road. Oftentimes, he confided, he dreamed of staying on a London-bound train and seeking out the woman he had loved and lost, the woman who had left him alone in a half-told story. In fifteen years, however, he had not made it east of the Tamar.

With a melancholy smile, he shook my hand and went to join in with the other travelling men and women who (with the surprising connivance of railway staff) had started playing tunes around a tin-can fire in the corner of the roundhouse.

The tune here presented is usually referred to as *Trematon Yard* and features Isaac St Cleer on third squeezebox.

Gwannhenwyn

Date recorded: August 31st, 1935

Performers: Downderry, Narkurs; Tregantle, Slim; Rosenannon, Sticks; Trebetherick, Endellion; Blackwater, Agnes; Portscatho, Solomon "Chips"; Chatagnier, Bou; Gunwalloe, Arthur "One Arm"; Lanhydrock, Reginald; Horingtops, Perranzabuloe; Unidentified, multiple.

Recordist: Valletort, Eric A.

Instruments: Concertina (treble and bass), harmonica (C), guitar, one row diatonic accordion, ukulele.

Setting: Temporary camp, Twelvetrees.

Tape number: EAV1822

Track number: 4

Archive ID: on.soundcloud.com/qkPLb

Technical note: Disc distortion (very severe). Static disruption of signal.

Notes on the session:

It is the nature, sadly, of field recording that sound quality is often not all that one might wish for. The current selection, universally catalogued as *Gwannhenwyn* is, for example, marred by static interference which I believe was caused by the proximity to my microphone of Arthur "One Arm"

Gunwalloe's hand hook. I include this piece, audio quality notwithstanding, as an example of the work of husband and wife duo Agnes Blackwater (on harmonica) and my sometime assistant Perranzabaloe Horningtops (on lead concertina). At the time of recording, Blackwater and Horningtops gave at least the appearance of living in the kind of harmony that their playing so often lacked; their path to this state of affairs however, appears to have been anything but straightforward.

Horningtops, a Falmouth longshoreman by trade, first came across Agnes when she visited the town with her father (the renowned Reverend Doctor Basil Blackwater) as part of his annual preaching circuit. Perranzabaloe watched awestruck as Agnes, standing behind her black-suited, bearded giant of a father, accompanied him with strident responses on her Hohner as he testified - her playing becoming ever more impassioned as the preacher worked himself into convulsions of fiery fury at the evils of the world. As father and daughter fell to their knees before the congregation in a final tear drenched climax of railing and wailing which only ended when neither could breathe for a second longer, Horningtops swore on all that was holy that he would not rest until he had made Agnes his wife. Securing Agnes's agreement to this plan was, I am told, surprisingly straightforward, gaining her father's consent considerably less so. His wrath at losing his daughter to a squeezebox playing roustabout was such that the young couple were left with no option but to elope, making good their escape by way of the last wagon of the Luxulyan Slow Pick Up. They were married in a quiet ceremony at Porkellis Friend's Hall presided over by Brother Minver Zelah (who accompanied the hymn singing on a bandoneon he had liberated from a Buenos Aires bordello whilst on missionary work).

For several years, it seems, Agnes and Perranzabaloe lived a contented if rootless life, working in the fields and playing for pennies on market days. When, however Horningtops was discovered to have taken up with the wife of the second assistant station master at St German's, Agnes contrived a rapprochement with her father who, with the help of a 12 gauge shot gun and a seven-man posse of lay preachers, convinced the philanderer that the flames of hell would be as nothing to the suffering he could expect should he stray from rectitude in future. Horningtops made firm and loud avowals to all who would hear that his ways had changed, and, following some tense renegotiation, he and Agnes returned to the strictures of their former life.

The seething resentment, bitterness and recrimination that flowed like sewage beneath the calm waters of the couple's apparent respectability can be heard in their playing throughout this piece as each tries to dislocate the song's tempo and to send the other the wrong way down overgrown and rusted musical sidings. They are accompanied by the flamboyant blind guitarist Endellion Trebetherick and his guide Arthur "One Arm" Gunwalloe on bass concertina (left side only).

Down Line Menheniot

Date recorded: July 18th, 1937

Performers: Trebetherick, Endellion; Bofarnel, Sweethouse; Smith, Trevarrian; Blazey, Camelford Jack; Ruthernbridge, Harold; Tremar, Darite; Gilmartin, "Pink" Lil; Luxulyan, Slim;; Burlawn, Ezra; Lanhydrock, Reginald; Unidentified, multiple.

Recordist: Valletort, Eric A.

Instruments: Harmonica (C), harmonica (Low F), one row diatonic accordion, homemade zither, concertina (treble and bass), ukulele, vox, cigar box banjo, percussion (improvised) various.

Setting: Main camp, Two Waters' Foot.

Tape number: EAV1845

Archive ID: https://on.soundcloud.com/jGzhZ

Technical note: Ambient interference. Disc distortion (severe).

Rights: Trad. arr Valletort

Notes on the session:

The recording here presented is blighted by, amongst many other things, the presence of Trevarrian Smith, Camelford Jack Blazey and Harold Ruthernbridge. The trio's insistence on contributing their brutish rhythm (played with sticks and metal tools on the first surface available) to any music being played around any camp fire they visited was to all intents and purposes insurmountable, and was a cause of much frustration to me as I searched in vain for evidence of grace or sensitivity amongst those I recorded. This frustration was shared by a number of players of quieter instruments including Mabyn St John, the relatively petite squeezebox doyenne, who was known on at least one occasion to have launched a concertina in the direction of one of the drummers' heads in protest at their inconsiderate tone and thoughtless volume.

The three men first met when they worked as deck hands on the trawler Our Jack out of Looe. For many years they toiled in harmony together, taking nightly to the waves in search of their silver prey, singing in strong workmanlike voices as they washed down the decks, and chanting lusty seaworn chanties as they hauled in the nets. Along the quaysides of Looe, the trio's strength in both body and in voice were widely celebrated. Sadly however, a night of drunken discord, the details of which are hard to ascertain but which may have involved cow theft, led to all three being discharged from their duties and led ultimately to their decision to take to the road.

Smith, Blazey and Ruthernford showed admirable loyalty to each other as they roamed the Cornish rails and byways; always seen together, and always with a song in their throats, they sought out the opportunities that the travelling life might bring. Like so many others during the period, the trio ended up making a precarious living on the shadowline between casual migrant labour and petty crime, working when they could and stealing only when necessary. In 1932 however, they were apprehended while in the act of attempting to break in to the Indian Queens sub post office. This offence was sufficient to earn them twelve months in Liskeard Gaol.

During their stay in prison, the three men came under the influence of long-term inmates who, having been banned from the use of musical instruments, had taught themselves to improvise rhythms using whatever tools were at hand. These inmates ridiculed the fishermen's tuneful harmonies and instead encouraged them to take up the asonic battering that echoed day and night around the prison walls. Smith, Blazey and Ruthernbridge, always somewhat suggestible, accepted this challenge with alacrity, and, due to their physical strength and restricted intelligence, found themselves well suited to the task. On their subsequent release, the trio took these rhythms (with a certain amount of misplaced pride) into the camps and hiding places of their fellow travellers where they were met with a reception that might be best described as lukewarm. All three, somewhat surprisingly, survived into old age.

This recording took place at Two Waters' Foot on the 18th July 1937. I include it only as an example of the result of allowing percussionists any degree of leeway and as a warning against those who still bleat incoherently in the defence of improvised instrumentation. To make matters worse, disgraced former stationmaster Sweethouse Bofarnel, who was lying on the ground next to my microphone, chose this moment to launch into a tirade that he referred to as a "train narration". In my notes, I refer to it as the random burblings of a dipsomaniac.

The Luxulyan Air or *Gonamena*

Date recorded: August 31st, 1938

Performers: Tregantle, Slim; Tremar, Darite; Rosenannon, Sticks; Trebetherick, Endellion; Gilmartin, "Pink" Lil; Luxulyan, Slim; Portscatho, Solomon "Chips"; Gunwalloe, Arthur; Chatagnier, Bou; Gunwalloe, Arthur "One Arm";; Johnson, Arwenack; Unidentified, multiple.

Recordist: Valletort, Eric A.

Instruments: Harmonica (C), harmonica (Low F), 3 stringed guitar (frutibox), one row diatonic accordion, homemade zither, concertina (treble and bass).

Setting: Transept, Church of St Petroc (decommissioned), Tregullon.

Tape number: EAV1887

Archive ID: on.soundcloud.com/YyU7h

Technical note: Some internal reverberation. Disc distortion (severe).

Rights: Trad. arr Valletort

Notes on the session:

One evening in the late summer of 1938, my sometime assistant Peranzabaloe Horningtops led me, via a tortuous and unnecessarily scenic route, to the abandoned church of

St Petroc at Tregullon. The building, deconsecrated in the late 1920s due to lack of a sustainable congregation and rumours of embezzlement amongst the clergy, was located on a steep hillside looking over the Glynn Valley not far from the Plymouth to Penzance main line. It was surrounded by thick woodland and was, by the time of my visit, in an overgrown and sadly dilapidated state.

According to Horningtops, the travelling men and women of the region had for many years been drawn towards this sacred building. Many was the night, apparently, that large numbers of vagabonds could be found within its precincts sheltering from bad weather beneath its leaking roof and sullying its hallowed halls with their ungodly musicianship as they awaited their next train or nefarious employment opportunity.

Upon our arrival on the evening in question, the sight that greeted us was, even to my experienced and worldly eyes, somewhat perturbing: a fire had been lit in what had formerly been the font, the few remaining pews were being broken up for fuel, men and women were sprawled about the transept in wantonly disrespectful poses, and a large oil can - presumably filled with strong liquor - was being passed from hand to filthy hand.

As the evening went on, more vagabonds arrived, many covered in the white dust of china clay wagons. Voices became louder, the oil can did a few more rounds, more sacred relics went in the fire, and the music making began. Despite my stern disapproval of the scene before me, I set up my equipment and began to record.

Amongst those present at this recording were: Slim Tregantle on harmonica, Arwenack Johnson on squeezebox, Sticks Rosenannon on 3 stringed fruitbox guitar, and Arthur "One Arm" Gunwalloe on baritone concertina. The piece here presented is a pedestrian reading of the *Luxulyan Air* or *Gonamena.* It was played at the end of the evening when the last of the liquor had been consumed and the last of the Bibles had been burned.

My visit to the church of St Petroc left me with a strong desire to cleanse myself of what I had seen and heard. As a result, I was inspired to write to the DCFDSS with a proposal to carry out research into the sacred music of Women's Institute choirs in the more affluent rural parishes of the South Hams. I have yet to receive their reply.

Lady of Lanreath

Date recorded: July 17th, 1937

Performers: Gilmartin, Pink Lil; Carharrick, Nancy; Boswell, Ernest "Big"; Constantine, Trevenan; Tregorrick, Slocan; Treviscoe, Little; Connoc, Bo; Carluddon, Crutches; Porkellis, "Blue" Bob; Boscarne, Blind; Unidentified, multiple.

Recordist: Valletort, Eric A.

Instruments: Ukulele, bass ukulele, 8 string box mandola, fishing reel banjo, concertina, bass concertina, soprano concertina, descant concertina, harmonica (low F), harmonica (high F poss), one row diatonic accordion.

Setting: Main camp, Two Waters' Foot

Tape number: EAV1889

Archive ID: on.soundcloud.com/wjRXz

Technical note: Ambient woodland sound, ambient railway noise, severe disc distortion.

Rights: Trad. arr Valletort

Notes on the session:

The piece here presented was, my notes remind me, recorded under highly stressful circumstances. The date was the 17th July 1937, and the location was Two Waters' Foot.

Upon my arrival, the scene was unremarkable enough - the sun was setting between the trees, long shadows stretched across the dusty earth of the camp, and around the central campfire were gathered a sizeable number of recumbent men and women of the road. The atmosphere, as I set up my recording equipment, appeared relatively convivial, with lewd comments, cigarettes and attempts at badinage being exchanged around the circle. As darkness fell, the music-making began in a restrained, and almost tasteful manner with Mabyn St John taking the lead on her descant concertina against a backdrop of birdsong and rustling leaves.

I was unable to capture this pleasantness, however, because before I had fully completed my pre-recording checks, the arrival of the late running Burngullow mixed-goods, and with it an influx of familiar and somewhat raucous vagabonds, had brought about a significant and unwelcome change to the camp's ambience. It became clear immediately that there was bad blood between several of the new arrivals and those who had previously had sole possession of the fire. My notes remind me, for example, that bass concertina player and sometime church warden "Blue" Bob Porkellis made immediately for Blind Boscarne upon his arrival, and then proceeded to aim a thunderous punch in the direction of the latter's throat. Boscarne, understandably enough, responded with a swinging melodeon to the face which left the verger briefly unconscious and the instrument short of several notes on the bass side. (Upon enquiry, I was later informed that the ill-feeling between the pair was deep-seated, long-running and was the result of a shared and utterly unrequited affection for "Crutches" Carluddon's unmarried sister).

Almost simultaneously, as I remember, a fight broke out between Lil Gilmartin and Nancy Carharrick with no apparent provocation on either side. This skirmish again involved the weaponization of free-reed instruments (in this case a punch-loading harmonica and the sharpened corner of a concertina end-plate), but was taken to another level when La Gilmartin pulled a log from the fire and attempted to brand a four-lettered obscenity onto her foe's forehead. It was only the intervention of Cyril "Hambone" Pentecost that prevented permanent injury to Nancy Carharrick, and serious offence to readers of a delicate sensibility.

Countless other squabbles and disputes simmered and erupted, and I began to fear that I might once again return from a field-recording expedition with nothing to show for my efforts. Then, as I watched Bo Connoc and Little Treviscoe rolling across the dirt in a cloud of flailing arms, legs, fists and ukuleles, I remembered the words of my late father, the eminent musicologist Sir Arthur Valletort: "Alcohol, my boy. Alcohol. It's the only language they understand." Inwardly rejoicing that I had come prepared, I reached into my bag and pulled out a bottle of single malt whisky and started to fill the grimy tin cups that were suddenly thrust towards me.

It would be wrong to suggest that harmony returned immediately to the camp, but the impact of my intervention was significant enough for me to be able to coral a number of musicians into something that, in extremis, one might describe as an ensemble. The ill-feeling that frothed barely below the surface can, however, be heard in all of the pieces recorded that night, and it came as no surprise that just after the finale of the here-presented piece, a cantankerous reading of the Dobwalls standard *Lady of Lanreath*, several further acts of random aggression and wanton instrumental clobbering broke out.

Finally, in a, perhaps ill-advised, attempt to refocus my subjects sufficiently to enable me to continue to record, I resorted to the bottle of absinthe that had been lying at the bottom of my bag since my ill-fated trip to the Loire Valley (an ultimately unsuccessful attempt to record the polyphonic chanting of retired grapetreaders) two summers previously. Again the tin cups were thrust towards me, and again I poured generously. The effect of this beverage had consequences too extreme to discuss here.

Nancegollan Road

Date recorded: 14th October 1936

Performers: Brown, Wheal Honey; Tremar, Darite; Horningtops, Perranzabaloe; Porkellis, Blue Bob; Gunwalloe, Arthur "One Arm"; Lanhydrock, Reginald; Luckett, Slow Jack; Portwrinkle, Blazey; Unidentified, multiple.

Recordist: Valletort, Eric A.

Instruments: Concertina, bass concertina, soprano concertina, ukulele, guitar, string bass, diatonic accordion, banjo, saw (possibly), harmonica, zither, percussion (various).

Setting: "Satan's Chapel" transient camp, nr St Ann's Chapel, East Cornwall.

Tape number: EAV1845

Track number: 17

Archive ID: on.soundcloud.com/fzuQn

Technical note: Disc distortion (severe).

About the session:

It was always something of a surprise to me that Blazey Portwrinkle survived as long as he did. His nonchalance in the face of oncoming rolling stock was legendary, and was matched only by his indifference to the profound offence that his words and deeds so often caused to his fellow travellers. Due to his exploits, many considered him a devil-may-care figure of romance; those of us blessed with a higher degree of perspicacity considered him rather less favourably. His tale, while in many senses inane and morally vacuous, is perhaps worth telling.

Born into stolid yeoman stock, Portwrinkle spent his early years assisting his father and mother on their small-holding just outside Herodsfoot, while at the same time earning a few extra pennies by caring for neighbours' livestock. His uncomplaining nature and apparent work ethic led to the widespread assumption that he would follow his parents' pathway towards the precarious yet respectable milieu of subsistence farming.

By the time he had reached his twenties, however, Portwrinkle had left such thoughts of stability behind and had "fallen in with a bad crowd", namely the infamous Trewoon Gang. Formed from the remnants of the Lanivet Disrespecters, and focused primarily on payroll robbery, this outfit were renowned both for the audacity of their operations and for their ability to cover large distances in short periods of time when making their escape. Blazey Portwrinkle, even while serving his initial apprenticeship, displayed qualities that marked him out as a rising star in this murky firmament. His seeming bravery, his disregard for the rule of law, and most of all his apparent lack of any sense of his own mortality soon became almost legendary. Many was the time that he was seen to board trains that others would not even consider approaching, and many was the time that he escaped the clutches of the law through the unlikely expedient of throwing himself between the wheels of moving wagons in order to evade his pursuers. The sight of young Portwrinkle disappearing into the starry night on the back of a screaming freight train with laughter on his lips and ill-gotten gains in his pockets became, for a brief period, an infuriatingly common one for the local constabulary.

Similar indifference towards his own safety was displayed by Portwrinkle in his dealings with the local underworld's hierarchy. On one occasion, for example, while sharing a wagon with Laughing Tony Tredinnick following a successful raid on the barrel factory at Doublebois, young Blazey took advantage of the older man's falling asleep to fleece him of his share in the takings. Upon awaking, Tredinnick quite naturally challenged Portwrinkle with regard to the missing loot before setting about him with a cold chisel. Witnesses recount how the younger man, rather than making any kind of admission or displaying any kind of remorse, let loose a volley of abuse in Laughing Tony's direction before throwing himself out of the wagon's open door onto the ballast below where he continued his diatribe. His insults, it is said, could still be heard on the wind several minutes and miles later.

Such incidents were apparently common. As a consequence, there were, by late 1936, said to be a not inconsiderable number of deeply serious characters desirous of causing Portwrinkle significant physical harm. It was regularly said at this time that if his own heedless spirit didn't kill him, there would be no shortage of volunteers to step in and complete the job.

In the end, however, Blazey Portwrinkle died in his sleep. In August 1937, while returning one night from a celebratory carousal at the Star and Plow in Boconnoc, the young man apparently felt the need to rest. Unaccountably (yet somehow typically) he chose to accomplish this by reclining across the tracks at Perranuthnoe Junction. Stupefied by alcohol, he lay his head on the rails, dared fate to do its worst, looked up at the stars, and began to dream of new adventures. The late running Kelly Bray goods then completed his story.

(His funeral, my notes remind me, was graced by sizeable numbers of distraught women loudly lamenting the passing of the man they held to be the dark-haired paragon of swashbuckling virtue. Other acquaintances who, like me, thought of him as nothing but an air-headed buffoon did not attend.)

Blazey Portwrinkle's ukulele can be heard on this rendition of Nancegollan Road captured at Satan's Chapel in October 1936.

Wheal Jenny

Date recorded: September 12th, 1938

Performers: Tremar, Darite; Trebetherick, Endellion; Connoc, Bo; Luckett, Jack (Slow); Treviscoe, Little; Constantine, Trevenan; Burlawn, Ezra; Boswell, Ernest "Big"; Tregorrick, Slocan; Carluddon, Crutches; Porkellis, "Blue" Bob; Unidentified, multiple.

Recordist: Valletort, Eric A.

Instruments: Oil can bass (homemade), ukulele, bass ukulele, 2 string guitar, homemade zither, copper wire banjo, concertina, bass concertina, soprano concertina, one row diatonic harmonica (low F), harmonica (high F).

Setting: Main sorting room, goods shed, Chilsworthy.

Tape number: EAV1867

Track number: 34

Archive ID: on.soundcloud.com/hE5dg

Technical note: Severe disc distortion.

Rights: Trad. arr Valletort

Notes on the session:

Lantic Levalsa grew up in a creekside shack on an eastern tributary of the Fowey river. He spent the days of his youth roaming the wooded hillsides of the valley, fishing the river's green waters, and digging for bait and driftwood at low tide. At 17 he acquired his first boat - a 12 foot ketch that, storm damaged and waterlogged, had washed up on a small shingle beach close to his home. With commendable determination and a degree of skill, the young man set about making this boat seaworthy once more and, after several months' labour, he was at last ready to set sail. He named the boat after his mother.

Following that day, Levalsa was seen only rarely at home. From before dawn until the depths of night, from Lostwithiel to the sea, he would roam the river alone, master of his craft, master of his destiny. He lived for the most part by fishing and ferrying, but he was certainly not above taking oysters from private beds or fish from others' nets, and he soon earned the reputation as the skipper to employ when a boat was needed for the earning of a less than honest shilling.

Then, one brilliantly sunny July afternoon in 1927 Lantic Levalsa's boat gently collided with the vessel belonging to a young lady by the name of Polly Pentewan. At the time, both sailors were in the shallows just off Penmarlam, and both were too busy looking for someone else's lobster pots to be keeping a proper look out. Their eyes met across the sparkling water. Levalsa had seen this young woman from a distance on previous occasions as she steered her small boat between the river traffic, and occasionally he had wondered about her. It was only now, however, as he stared at the beauty of her face and her golden hair flashing in the reflected sunlight, that he saw with perfect clarity that his heart's lonely voyage was at an end. Together the pair untangled their craft and together they resumed their illicit activity.

For the rest of that summer Polly and Levalsa sailed together the length and breadth of the river. Levalsa soon found out that the woman beside him was just as skilled a boat handler as he, and just as capable of finding new and nefarious ways of raising funds. When resting from their labours, the pair would drag their boats onto the sand of tiny secluded coves and would lie in the sun talking of their next adventure. Many times Levalsa was on the point of putting into words his heart's longing as he stared across the sand at his beautiful companion.

Fate, however, intervened when one night Levalsa happened to call into the Prince of Prussia for a thirst-quencher before floating home. As he stood at the bar he looked absently around the room. And there in the gloom of the furthest corner, was Polly Pentewan in the arms of renowned womaniser and ferryman Tregorrick Duporth.

Crushed and heartbroken, Levalsa returned to his boat. Instead of crossing the river towards home, he drifted slowly upstream. Lying in the stern sheets he looked up at the stars as the tide carried him ever further from the woman he loved. Eventually he came ashore at Golant.

Details are vague from this point onwards, but it would appear that Levalsa soon fell in with a band of tramps and soon joined them on their aimless journeying. Like so many others, he then proceeded to spend the next decades roaming from town to town, drinking to excess, doing what he could to survive, and regaling anyone who would listen with the details of his misfortunes.

The rather unfortunate conclusion to this tale was disclosed to me on the night of the here-presented recording by "Slow" Jack Luckett (who can be heard struggling unsuccessfully with the chord changes in the second verse).

One night, so the story goes, Levalsa finally decided to return to Fowey to at last declare his love to Polly Pentewan regardless of the consequences. Witnesses describe how he spent the evening in the Prince before going in search of his beloved. Unable to find her, he continued drinking and finally ended up on the quayside looking out across the star-streaked expanse of the river. A boat drifted past, silver in the moonlight. Suddenly, Levalsa called out across the water, apparently convinced that at the wheel of this boat was his golden-haired treasure. Apparently convinced also that she was calling him to her for a love drenched reunion. Without hesitation Lantic Levalsa threw aside his bottle, jumped into the water and began to swim towards the silver sails. With predictably tragic results.

The people of Penmarlam still talk of the man whose love was so strong he would risk everything to cross the salt water to reach the woman of his dreams. Many also still remember the golden haired girl who eventually sold her boat, married well and dedicated her subsequent leisure time to jam making and the Women's Institute.

Sibblyback Strut

Date recorded: August 14th, 1935

Performers: Porkellis, "Blue" Bob; Rosecraddock, Jago "Red Eye"; Trelissick, Bob "Washboard"; Trebetherick, Endellion; Kilhallon, Trethowel; Kilhallon, Geevor;; Treviscoe, Little; Unidentified, multiple.

Recordist: Valletort, Eric A.

Instruments: Steel string guitar, concert ukulele, bass ukulele, homemade fuse wire zither, 3 string banjo, concertina, bass concertina, concertina (damaged), one row diatonic accordion, harmonica (high F), string bass (metal bucket body).

Setting: 3rd Hovel, Baptist Street Migrant Camp.

Tape number: EAV1752

Archive ID: on.soundcloud.com/wr8Pj

Technical note: Ambient interference, locomotive movements (close quarters), disc distortion.

Rights: Trad. arr Valletort

Notes on the session:

Throughout my career in ethnomusicology, I have consistently displayed the utmost respect and consideration for my colleagues, however negligible their talents or wrongheaded their opinions. An exception to this generous attitude, however, has to be made in the case of The Reverend Ernest Barrington who, on innumerable occasions, has tested my forbearance beyond any reasonable limits.

Despite lacking any formal musicological qualification, Barrington decided as a young man that the study of country dance in and around his parish would be a profitable way to fill the many leisure hours that his employment allowed. Notebook in hand and pipe in mouth, he would while away his days wandering the byways and listening out for the sound of free reeds and stamping feet. His subsequent descriptions of white-dressed maidens and sturdy ploughboys taking part in traditional flower dances were florid, overwritten and technically inaccurate. They were also, however, unaccountably popular with the same journal editors who were so consistently dismissive of my own work.

Lest it should be thought that professional jealousy is at the heart of my ill-feeling towards Barrington, however, I feel compelled to share a single example of the deviousness that was so typical of the man. In the midsummer heat of 1935, I came across Barrington in the saloon bar of The White Hart in Harrowbarrow. Apparently all generosity, he invited me to half a bitter and asked me the direction of my research. When I told him that it was my intention to leave the study of vagabond musicians and instead to focus my talents on something more worthy, he clapped me on the back and told me of a place he had come across that should be my first port of call. In golden words he described a location where sweet and sanctified English melodies, unsullied by worldly influence, were played by instrumental artisans and given wings by pure maiden voices. Where pastoral music, almost holy in its beauty, was offered up to the sweet scented winds by honest and innocent rural folk. Where, in short, I would find what I had sought for so long. Much excited, I asked Barrington where I should find this place. He told me to head for Upton Cross and ask anyone there for directions to Baptist Street.

I should perhaps have gauged from the giggling and askance reaction from the first person of whom I asked this question upon my arrival at Upton, that something was amiss. However, I followed unquestioningly the route I was given, and soon found myself carrying my heavy recording equipment along a dusty path heading away from the village towards the railway tracks. The evening was warm and close. While walking, a sense of dread grew within me as I began to be aware of strange sounds and unpleasant smells in the air. I rounded a bend in the path; ahead of me was the silhouette of a small gathering of the meanest huts and shacks imaginable lining the railway tracks and blocking the evening sunlight from view. Dogs barked, children screamed and black smoke from passing locomotives floated in billowing waves between the buildings. Tin cans, torn clothes and empty cigarette packets lay strewn across the soot-encrusted floor. On the side of the first hovel I came to were painted the words: Baptist Street.

I looked along the tracks. Seated on a wooden crate in front of an oil drum fire in the smoky evening light was a silhouetted figure playing a guitar. I immediately recognised this man as Red Eye Rosecraddoc. Aware of his reputation and of his lengthy criminal record, I decided that this was the moment to turn on my heel and leave this forsaken spot. As I turned however, I was greeted by the sight of Geevor and Trethowel Kilhallon (Wheal Honey Brown's semi-feral step-children) who had noted my arrival and were now moving threateningly towards me, harmonicas in hand.

Without saying a word, they ushered me back towards the fire and motioned me to set up my recording equipment. In the time it took me to do this, we were joined by numerous other desperate looking characters carrying a variety of battered and smoke-blackened instruments. These men formed an intimidating circle around me and I was not permitted to leave until I had recorded an entire evening's worth of their predictably appalling output.

(The tune here presented was chosen for being the least offensive result of the Baptist Street session - largely because Cutcrew Tregonna had fallen into a drunken stupor by this stage and was no longer able to contribute his home-made hurdy-gurdy to the ensemble.)

Naturally, as a result of this episode I reported the Reverend Barrington to the DCFDSS for his unacceptable breach of ethnomusicological ethics, demanding that he should, at the very least, be disbarred for life. Almost incredibly, their reply intimated that I should "grow a sense of humour".

Stony Creek Moan

Date recorded: August 5th 1938

Performers: Trevevva, Charles "Burnthouse"; Unidentified; Unidentified.

Recordist: Valletort, Eric A.

Instruments: Concertina, baritone (possibly bass) concertina, plucked ukulele.

Setting: New Street Ope, Plymouth.

Tape number: EAV1812

Track number: 7b

Archive ID: on.soundcloud.com/E2oBs

Technical note: Some severe disc distortion.

Notes on the session:

As Buenos Aires was to the accordionists from the plains of rural Argentina, as Chicago was to the harmonica players from the dusty byways of the Mississippi Delta, and as Lisbon was to the guitarists from the quiet pueblos of central Portugal, so Plymouth was to the troubadours from the green hills and wooded valleys west of the Tamar.

Like so many of the destitute wayfarers who habituated the roads and rails of Cornwall in the 1930s, Charles "Burnthouse" Trevevva eventually found himself drawn towards the city's bright lights and dubious pleasures. A man of some intelligence and a certain shabby elegance, he dropped off a china clay train at King's Road station in late 1935, before making his way to the Barbican where he eventually gained employment as a porter in the fish market. This line of work, however, quickly became irksome, and it was not long before Trevevva dedicated himself fully to his twin lifelong passions: the bottle and the squeezebox.

The flickering sight of his silhouette soon became a familiar one on the cobbled corners and alleyways running down to the harbour. At night, his dark hat and crumpled suit would throw angular shadows across the stones as he played mournful tunes for passersby. In front of him, his meagre takings sparkled on a stolen collection plate; beside him on the pavement stood a whisky bottle, empty by the end of the night.

Little in the way of further biographical detail is known about Charles Trevevva, despite the many years he spent among the Barbican's tangle of streets, bars, bait shops and bordellos. He was rarely seen by day, his abode was not fixed, and he spoke only to a few other citizens of the night. The sole certainty was that as daylight faded into darkness and the streets began to fill with the roaring waves of carousers, his frail figure would appear and the sparse notes of his concertina would begin to float above the noise.

It was always said that Trevevva had lost his heart many years ago to a lady of the night he met when he first came to the city. One evening, so the story goes, he proposed to her beneath a lamppost at the corner of Southside Street. She replied that she would give him her answer the following night. At the appointed time Trevevva waited beneath the same lamppost. He heard her laughter from the dark end of the street. Her footsteps approached, high heels on the cobbles. Arm in arm with a sailor, she passed him by.

My chance to record Charles Trevevva came in the early hours of the morning of 5th August 1938. In the narrow darkness of a side street he played tune after tune without stopping, without talking. For some of the evening he was accompanied by two unidentified musicians who, without words, sat down and joined him. His hat, pulled down low over his eyes, covered his expression as he played. Only once, when he heard the tread of high heels on the cobbles, did he look up. I watched as the light from the distant lamp on Southside street illuminated the change from hope to sorrow on his features when the footsteps faded.

"Burnthouse" Trevevva remained a somewhat enigmatic figure, wedded to the darkness, almost unknown, until he finally disappeared from view one bitterly cold winter's night. Few remarked upon his absence or noticed the hat and empty whisky bottle left by the bins at the end of a narrow alleyway behind the Customs House. My notes remind me that his concertina was last heard on New Year's Eve 1939. His beloved's heels (and her laughter) had, incidentally, fallen silent two days previously.

Tresillian Fields

Date recorded: August 26th, 1937

Performers: Treviscoe, Little; Honey Brown, Wheal; Stepaside, Josiah "Tin Joe"; Lanhydrock, Reginald; Nanstallon, Sonny Boy; Boswell, Ernest "Big"; Pentecost, Cyril "Hambone"; Amble, Chapel; Nancledra Towedrack; Horningtops, Perranzabaloe; Carluddon, "Crutches"; Boscarne, Blind; Luckett, Jack "Slow"; Doublebois, Enric; Doublebois, Aleric; Unidentified, several.

Recordist: Valletort, Eric A.

Instruments: 4 string guitar, fruitbox guitar, ukulele, bass ukulele, zither, concertina, concert concertina, soprano concertina, bass concertina (x2?), copper wire banjo, harmonica (low F or B flat), one row diatonic accordion (Caradon tuning).

Setting: Main camp, Two Waters' Foot

Tape number: EAV1898

Archive ID: on.soundcloud.com/C29Uv

Technical note: Ambient sound, disc distortion.

Notes on the session:

Born into poverty in the wilds of the Roseland peninsula, Josiah "Tin Joe" Stepaside had run away to sea before the age of fifteen. Serving as a deckhand on crabbing boats, barges and trawlers, he quickly gained a reputation for reliability, strength, and even sobriety. He also became known for his skill with cards - many was the crewman that ended a trip in debt to the young shipmate who had appeared so naïve and who had turned out to have such a sharp eye for the high wild hand.

Perhaps not surprisingly, this success led to resentment and, ultimately, violence. One evening, whilst awaiting the turning of the tide in the upper reaches of the Lynher, Tin Joe was set upon by three of his crewmates following a hotly contested game of pinochle. As a result of the ensuing fracas, the young tar eventually washed up with two black eyes and a broken arm on the shores of the river at Whacker Quay.

To his great good fortune, the bruised and battered sailor was found by a limpet picker by the name of Nancy Carharrack. This young woman (who had likewise left at home at an early age) tended to Tin Joe's wounds, fed him from her own meagre provisions and found him shelter in a netmender's loft. He recovered quickly and, following many evenings' heartfelt discussion by the light of a fish-oil lamp, the pair decided to leave their former lives of relatively honest work behind and to throw their fortunes to the vicissitudes of the road.

With Nancy's distracting good looks and Tin Joe's acuity, the pair quickly found a profitable line of business, to wit: parting the drunk from their money in every public house and roadside inn from Bodmin to St Blazey. For many months the pair lived in happiness and profligacy as a result of their immoral earnings - travelling from town to town in a stolen Wolesley, laying down their crooked cards and revelling in the freedom of their new life. Every sunset offered them a new prospect, and every dawn promised a new adventure.

Once again, however, natural justice, with righteous and crushing inevitability, was eventually served. One night in Lansallos, a railway worker took umbrage when Tin Joe played his fifth queen, and set about the former sailor with a broken bottle. The police were called and, after a brief struggle, they removed young Stepaside to the cells. When brought before the judge the next day, Tin Joe discovered to his dismay that Nancy Carharrack had taken the first opportunity to absent herself, and was now long gone.

Upon his eventual release, a heartbroken and embittered Tin Joe fell in with a crowd of railway tramps and took to the vagabond life. His former skills did not desert him, but as few of those against whom he played had any possessions with which to gamble, the cards in his hand now held little interest for him. He did, however, once win a battered and wheezing concertina from Blind Trezaise in a rigged and drunken game at Foxhole Junction. As can be heard from the here presented recording (the standard *Tresillian Fields* captured by myself at Two Waters' Foot in August 1937), Tin Joe made only the most cursory of attempts to learn to play it.

Lady Relubbus

Date recorded: June 19th, 1937

Performers: Brown, Wheal Honey; Zelah, Minver; Tregillis, Seth "Wheel Nut"; Quintrell, Harold "Red"; Trebetherick, Endellion; Boswell, Ernest "Big"; Tregantle, Slim; Luxulyan, Slim; Tremar Darite; Carluddon, "Crutches"; Unidentified, multiple.

Recordist: Valletort, Eric A.

Instruments: Concertina, second concertina, third concertina (poss), bass concertina, one-row diatonic, tin-can zither, ukulele, banjo, guitar, harmonica (various).

Setting: Third arch from the left, Truro Station Approach viaduct.

Tape number: EAV1876

Track number: 14

Archive ID: on.soundcloud.com/pAZe1

Technical note: Ambient noise, severe disc distortion.

Notes on the session:

Seth "Wheel Nut" Tregillis sold his soul to the devil at the disused water tank just outside St Columb Minor in late August 1932. This at least was his contention. According to the account that was later shared around every campfire in Cornwall, Tregillis had been approached by a tall, besuited man with no shadow who interrupted him while he was busking outside the post office in Nancledra. After the briefest of preambles, this man asked the young vagabond if he wished to become the true master of the concertina he held between his hands. "Wheel Nut" replied that he most certainly did, particularly as that day's takings had been so disappointing. Arrangements were made, and the following night, at the appointed time, Tregillis made his way to the water tank at St Columb. A full moon shone through the thick mist, and the only sound was the swaying of a rusted signal arm in the breeze. Just before midnight, a guard's lantern, showing red, came swinging along the tracks towards him.

Tregillis would never say what happened next. He would, however, claim that from that night forward his luck changed. His street corner performances were no longer treated with apathy or disdain, he was regularly showered with coins from appreciative listeners, and he was never again forcibly removed from a town for his own safety. His "triumphs" with the fairer sex (a subject about which Tregillis was tiresomely eager to talk) also became ever more numerous and ever more outlandishly implausible, presumably as a by-product of the unholy transaction.

Like all right-thinking ethnomusicologists, I of course treat such tales with the contempt they deserve. The Faustian pact has no place in serious socio-historical cultural research. In Tregillis's case, he was a musician of small talent and a large mouth. His tales of financial and romantic success were unsupported by any physical evidence, and to anyone who listened to his playing (he appears on lead Lachenal in this 1937 recording of *Lady Relubbus*), the very idea that he had paid such a high price for such a meagre return seems utterly ludicrous.

The vast majority of his travelling companions, however, appeared beguiled by his tales: word of his pact spread to the four corners of the peninsula and, at every camp and waiting place he would be received with something approaching awe by the uneducated throng with whom he shared the road. When questioned about his dealings with the forces of darkness, he would reply with alacrity and in ever greater detail. Many of his listeners expressed surprise that one with such a sentence hanging over him should appear so garrulous and full of good cheer. The more perceptive amongst them made the link between these traits and his prodigious gin consumption.

One night in 1938, Seth "Wing Nut" Tregillis left the camp at Fourlanesend saying he was going to meet an old friend. He did not return.

Chilsworthy Girl

Date recorded: August 6th, 1935

Performers: Gunwalloe, Arthur; Chatagnier, Bou; Pentecost, Cyril "Hambone"; Burlawn, Ezra; Unidentified strikers, multiple.

Recordist: Valletort, Eric A.

Instruments: Concertina, bass concertina, ukulele, guitar, string bass, diatonic accordion, banjo, clackers, spoons, forks, harmonica.

Setting: Workers' Camp, Tregarrick's Apple Farm, Menheniot.

Tape number: EAV1871

Track number: 32

Archive ID: on.soundcloud.com/VDh2H

Technical note: Severe disc distortion, microphone interference from players and dancers.

Notes on the session:

The agricultural workers' strike of August 1935 centred on the Pendogget parish and was primarily caused by the irresponsible actions of one man - Lawrence Arthur St James.

Born into considerable wealth, St James was brought up amongst the parks and stucco terraces of Kensington, and was educated at a number of prestigious public schools. However, a streak of wilful oppositionalism (alongside a somewhat suspicious love of literature) became apparent in the young St James as his school years passed and, to the horror of his parents and all right-thinking onlookers, he rejected the berth at Lloyds of London that had been set aside for him and instead chose to join the Socialist Workers' Party. Worse was to follow when, in late 1934, St James informed his parents that he was setting off on a tour of Welsh coal mines in order to help organise striking miners.

On his return to London, those close to him tried again to redirect his footsteps towards a more worthwhile use of his talents. St James, however, could talk only of injustice and poverty, of workers being ground down by capital, of the true dignity of labour, and other such Bolshevistic gibberish; it came as no real surprise, therefore, when, weeks later, he announced that he was embarking on a new tour of troublemaking - this time in order to support the cause of migrant agricultural workers.

The evening of 6th August 1935 was much like many others I had come across on my travels. I had chosen to base myself and my recording apparatus at a camp between the railway line and Tregarrick's apple farm, in the unlikely hope that among the several hundred men and women who were engaged with the harvest and who had made this camp their temporary home, I might find a handful whose musicianship would prove worthy of being kept for posterity. Congratulating myself on my seemingly indomitable optimism, I set up my equipment, took my sandwiches from my hamper, and prepared to wait.

At last the sun set, and the fruit pickers began to make their way back from the fields. To a man they were covered from head to foot in dust and sweat; they walked with a weary, almost broken gate, limping into camp on ruined shoes before finally falling heavily into their place by the fire. They spoke little as they rummaged amongst their possessions for something to eat. They then sat in silence with their meagre repast. Many had hands reddened with blooded wounds, and many appeared utterly shattered by their poverty and their day's labour. I began to despair of being able to accomplish any sort of worthwhile recording.

A car's approach along the dusty farm track broke the quiet of the scene. Two men got out. One of them (Lawrence St James, I later ascertained) stood on a wooden crate and began to address the assembled throng. As his educated tones mingled with the birdsong and the crackling of the fire, a number of men summoned the energy to raise themselves and to approach where he stood, and within minutes he was addressing a large, and apparently very receptive, crowd.

The thrust of St James's speech was based, predictably enough, on the premise that the farmers were exploiting the labourers and were making huge profits by paying starvation wages. This of course drew waves of full-throated agreement from the throng, which St James capitalised on by proposing that everyone present should refuse to return to the fields until workers' conditions had been improved. Loud cheers followed, and a delegation was quickly sent to inform the farm owners of the decision to strike.

The men and women around the fire, who a few short minutes previously had appeared lifeless and bereft of hope, now appeared transformed. The camp became a bustle of activity, laughter and noise, and as darkness fell, all present gathered around the fire to drink, to hear more speeches predicting the end of their sorrows, and finally to indulge in what might loosely be described as music. Relieved that my journey had not been entirely wasted, and despite my strong distaste for any and all industrial action, I began to record. (Conditions were far from ideal and the constant buffeting of my microphone by over-enthusiastic players and dancers can be heard throughout the piece from the session presented here).

The communal, and delusional, euphoria of that night was short-lived, however. Early the following morning, the farm owners took advantage of the workers' collective hangover to induce a number of them to return to work with the promise of a slightly increased cider ration. Others soon followed, and by midday, the entire workforce was back in the fields.

By this time Lawrence St James had left Pendogget and had moved on to cause more needless vexation elsewhere. On his return to London a few months later, he wrote a book about his Cornish experiences and about the hardships and injustice he had supposedly witnessed. This work was highly praised in both radical and literary circles, but, ever one to swim against the tide, I had had no need to read it in order to feel assured of the derisible quality of its thesis.

I Knew Not

Date recorded: May 28th, 1938

Performers: Treviscoe, Little; Pentecost, Cyril "Hambone"; Treseder, Daubuz; Gunwalloe, Arthur "One Arm"; Connoc, Bo; Luckett, Jack; Tolvaddon, Jonah; Porkellis, "Blue" Bob; Unidentified, three.

Recordist: Valletort, Eric A.

Instruments: Twine string guitar, vocal, ukulele, bass ukulele, 4 string banjo, concertina, bass concertina, retuned harmonica (Callington temper), harmonica (high F).

Setting: Main camp, Two Waters' Foot.

Tape number: EAV1856

Track number: 13

Archive ID: on.soundcloud.com/WrqTo

Technical note: Ambient interference, disc distortion.

Rights: Melody Trad. arr Valletort; lyrics Tolvaddon.

Notes on the session:

There are a number of theories as to how Jonah Tolvaddon ended up spending the final years of his life writing poetry in an abandoned lineside hut by the Sandy Lane level crossing on the ridge above Calstock. There is, however, general consensus about his early career. Following an unhappy adolescence working as a knocker in the Wheal Jenny mine, Tolvaddon, commentators agree, left for London where he became embroiled in the outer fringes of the criminal underworld. This, it would appear, principally involved providing "muscle" for a largely unsuccessful gang of extorters in and around Shepherds Bush Market. While in Wormwood Scrubs following his inevitable incarceration, Tolvaddon fell under the benign influence of the prison chaplain, spending many hours talking to this worthy divine about the poor decisions he had taken in his life thus far and, at great length and in intricate detail, about the verdant beauty of the land he had left behind. Upon his release he wasted no time in returning to the Tamar Valley where he found, at least initially, the emerald Eden he had remembered.

Securing work on the quayside at Danescombe, Jonah Tolvaddon passed a number of years in quiet contentment, spending his meagre wage on the necessities of life, taking long walks through the steep sided valley, and apparently becoming a relatively upright member of society.

And here the trail goes somewhat cold. At some point between the summers of 1935 and 1936, an incident or incidents occurred that led Tolvaddon to abandon both work and home, and led him inexorably towards a life of poetry and seclusion. Cider, women, poverty and various forms of criminality have all been suggested as motives behind his move to the remote lineside hut, but such speculation remains unconfirmed. When questioned, Tolvaddon would never specify the cause of this rupture in his life's pathway, and his verse (for the most part predictably morose, derivative piffle) gives similarly few clues. My notes from my single visit to his hut talk of his stillness as he sat over his work at a rickety wooden table, and of his melancholy as he mumbled quiet words to himself and stared out of the smashed window across the tracks towards the folds of the valley below.

Intermittently, he would leave his hut and would join other men and women of the road on their travels. The recording here presented was made when he appeared at Two Waters' Foot one evening in June 1938. Towards the end of the night, a relatively subdued piece was being played and Tolvaddon, without being asked, began to intone one of his works. As I was unable to stop the recording in time, his words have been kept for posterity.

(Jonah Tolvaddon was found deceased in his hut a few years after this recording took place. A poem lay unfinished on his table and his gaze was fixed on the folds of the green fields before him.)

Cardinham to Lanivet

Date recorded: June 19th 1937

Performers: Carluddon, Crutches; Boswell, Ernest "Big"; Constantine, Trevenan; Tregorrick, Slocan; Porkellis, "Blue" Bob; Lanhydrock, Reginald; Treviscoe, Little; Unidentified, multiple.

Recordist: Valletort, Eric A.

Instruments: Ukulele, bass ukulele, 8 string guitar, homemade zither, fence wire banjo, concertina, bass concertina, soprano concertina, harmonica (low F), harmonica (high F poss), one row diatonic.

Setting: Main camp, Two Waters' Foot.

Tape number: EAV1814

Track number: 2

Archive ID: on.soundcloud.com/JesNV

Technical note: Background ambience, severe disc distortion.

Rights: Trad. arr Valletort

Notes on the session:

One Saturday in early June 1937, I was making my way towards Merrymeet, a small village located in rolling green hills a few miles beyond Liskeard. I was anxious to make good time, as the reason for my journey, namely the village's Goose Fair, was due to commence at noon. The centrepiece of this celebration was the Gooseherd's Wassail - a country dance, possibly pagan in origin, performed annually by the maidens and unmarried young men of the locality. I had for many years dreamed of recording and analysing this rather obscure and unheralded event, and of subsequently sharing my findings with the London-based cognoscenti of folk song and dance (who, it would be fair to say, had hitherto been somewhat dismissive of my work).

As I drove between high hedges on the dusty white country lanes that led towards Merrymeet, I pictured the scene that awaited me: the village bedecked in floral tributes, coloured ribbons fluttering in the warm wind beneath a cloudless blue sky, white-dressed maidens with freshly cut flowers in their hair dancing freely with apple-cheeked young farmhands on the soft green grass, church bells peeling, the village elders supping warm beer and looking on appreciatively as they remembered their own younger days, local musicians accompanying the dance with faultless accuracy and impeccably good taste. My thoughts, sadly, were then interrupted by a loud report and the realisation that my nearside front tyre had punctured.

With the help of a passing tractor driver, I was able to fit the spare wheel in under half an hour. By the time I reached Merrymeet however, I could see immediately that the wassail was already underway and was in fact reaching its climax. As quickly as I could, I unloaded my recording equipment and hurried with it under my arms towards the village green. Maddeningly, in the time it took to set up and prepare my Marconi to record, the music had finished and the dancers had frolicked away to continue their celebrations elsewhere. To compound my aggravation, I was then accosted by The Reverend Ernest Barrington, amateur musicologist, rector of Rosenannon parish church and possessor of considerably less folkloric knowledge than he routinely gave himself credit for, who feigned sympathy for my circumstances and asked me, with clearly malicious intent, whether I would like to listen to the recording he had just made of the dance.

On my way home to Middle Taphouse, I stopped briefly at Two Waters' Foot and, in search of some minor consolation, made the recording here presented - a shambolic reading of the call and response Restormel worksong *Cardinham to Lanivet.* Upon my arrival, a large ensemble was gathered around the fire and the prevailing mood was not a pleasant one. Several bottles of stolen whisky had clearly made their way into the camp, a number of fights were taking place simultaneously, and every few minutes a train would pass, more tramps would arrive and new enmities would be made. As I looked around at the filthily clad, dirty-faced humanity before me, and as I listened to the shoddy and uneducated musicianship they produced, my feelings of bitterness with regard to the day's events remained in all senses unassuaged.

Reverend Barrington's treatise on the Merrymeet Wassail appeared in the July edition of the Devon and Cornwall Folk Dance and Song Society Journal. It contained a number of factual inaccuracies that I dutifully highlighted in a letter to the journal's editor.

Lifton Rain

Date recorded: September 12th, 1938

Performers: Tremar, Darite; Trebetherick, Endellion; Connoc, Bo; Luckett, Jack (Slow); Treviscoe, Little; Constantine, Trevenan; Trispen, Ezra; Tregorrick, Slocan; Carluddon, Crutches; Porkellis, “Blue” Bob; Unidentified, multiple.

Recordist: Valletort, Eric A.

Instruments: Oil can bass, ukulele, bass ukulele, 4 string guitar, copper wire banjo, concertina, bass concertina, soprano concertina, one row diatonic harmonica (low F), harmonica (high F).

Setting: Main sorting room, goods shed, Chilsworthy.

Tape number: EAV1867

Track number: 32

Archive ID: on.soundcloud.com/BQSmm

Technical note: Disc distortion.

Rights: Trad. arr Valletort

Notes on the session:

Ezra Trispen was one of the more cerebral men of the road I encountered on my musicological odyssey. His appearance was that of an oversized farmhand of the basest type, yet his ability to discourse on a breadth of subjects in detail and at length was such that one soon forgot his obvious uncleanliness and unpleasant odour and became involuntarily entangled in his words' intricate web.

Just where Trispen acquired this knowledge and apparent effortless eloquence was something of a mystery. He was widely believed to have been born into a stolid working class family in the Tresillian mining belt around 1908, but little is known about the years between his childhood and his appearance beside the campfire at Roche Junction in 1935. Some reports suggest that his inherent intelligence enabled him to secure a place at one of Cornwall's great seats of learning; others suggest the more likely possibility that he used whatever literature was at his disposal (most probably through the municipal lending library at St Columb Minor) to fill his brain with vast quantities of indiscriminately arranged fact. What was indisputable, however, was that this apparent intellect came accompanied by profound social awkwardness and substantial mental instability (the latter not helped by a penchant for drinking shoe polish).

These facets of his character manifested themselves, according to police records, in numerous stays at the Duchy's correctional facilities. Trispen's crimes were not overly serious it would appear, and tended to involve scaring people through sudden bursts of irrational behaviour rather than anything more premeditated. However, he was, by the age of thirty, a seasoned recidivist with several years' experience as a prison librarian under his belt.

A further consequence of one of his lengthier stays at Liskeard was the large 4 stringed guitar given him by Arthur "Chisel" Polhawn in recognition of his services in reading and replying to letters from the latter's serially unfaithful spouse. As with other aspects of his self-improvement, Trispen set about learning to play this instrument with single-minded determination. Sadly, however, this determination could not overcome the dual handicaps of his sausage-like fingers and his massive body's inherent lack of coordination. The upshot of this was that his guitar playing was so loud, and so rarely tuneful that his fellow prisoners on more than one occasion resorted to violently unpleasant methods to silence it.

Upon his release, Trispen took the disastrously unrealistic decision to attempt to make a living as an itinerant musician. For the next few years his huge frame would be seen lumbering along the peninsula's byways, guitar slung over his mighty shoulders, on his way to the next town and its unsuspecting citizenry. Once established on an appropriately central street corner, he would embark upon his thunderous, and nosebleed-inducingly monotonous, repertoire. That the audience reaction to his work was overwhelmingly negative, and that he barely made enough money to avoid starvation on his travels, was wholly unsurprising.

Salvation appeared in the petite, yet determined and resourceful form of Miss Anna St Budeaux. This worthy young woman had recently established, in one of the cobbled alleyways near Plymouth's harbour, a small, fiercely literary, bookshop outside which, one afternoon, Ezra Trispen set up his stall to play. Although naturally repulsed by his music, the young bookseller was sufficiently sympathetic to the tramp's obviously pitiful plight to invite him into the shop for warmth and a cup of tea. Within minutes of Trispen's entering the shadowy heart of this temple to the written word, and within moments of his embarking upon a discourse of profound and sensitive authority on the works filling the shelves around him, Miss Anna's feelings of sympathy (and mild distaste at his appearance) were replaced by fascination and in due course by emotions of a far deeper kind.

These sentiments were eventually discovered to be awkwardly mutual, and the sight of the huge, roadworn vagabond walking arm in arm with the delicate flower of Plymouth's literary community soon became a common one. Furthermore, Trispen's rough-hewn wisdom and tales of the coarser side of life proved immediately and immensely popular amongst the young artistic community that coalesced around Miss Anna's shop, and many was the evening he spent as the centre of earnest attention in the cafés and terraces of the quarter. At the end of such evenings Ezra would always reach for his guitar and offer to serenade the gathering in his own inimitable style. With gentle kindness, however, Miss Anna would at such moments place the instrument out of his reach and would whisper something quietly about needing to get an early night.

For one spring and one summer Trispen and Miss Anna lived their bizarrely compatible lives together amongst the bookshelves. By Autumn, however, the call of the road, and the stubborn and misguided belief that people wanted to hear his music, led Ezra to return to his former existence. He died in predictable penury a few years later.

Ever the pragmatist, Miss Anna soon overcame any feelings of abandonment she may have experienced, and a year later married a surrealist poet from Buckland Monochorum.

Higher Kelly

Date recorded: July 14th, 1937

Performers: Trebetherick, Endellion; Bofarnel, Sweethouse; Washaway, Cubert; Ruthernbridge, Harold; Tremar, Darite; Gilmartin, "Pink" Lil; Luxulyan, Slim; Portscatho, Solomon "Chips"; Polkerris, Bob, "Blue"; Gunwalloe, Arthur; Connoc, Bo; Coppa, Bos; Burlawn, Ezra; Lanhydrock, Reginald; Unidentified, multiple.

Recordist: Valletort, Eric A.

Instruments: Harmonica (C), harmonica (Low F), one row diatonic accordion, concertina (treble and bass), ukulele, bass (bucket/mop construction), percussion (improvised) various.

Setting: Main dining room, The Railway Hotel, Trethawle.

Tape number: EAV1889

Archive ID: on.soundcloud.com/u5dGQ

Technical note: Ambient interference. Disc distortion (severe).

Rights: Trad. arr Valletort

Notes on the session:

The Railway Hotel in Trethawle was not, by the late 1930s, a place that any respectable traveller would ever choose to frequent. Perhaps because of this, it was one of the few places that would permit men and women of the road to take up temporary residence. My sometime guide Perranzabuloe Horningtops had on many occasions recommended that I visit the establishment, speaking in tones of hushed awe of the music he had on occasion heard there - music made by an assembled vagabond throng in the hotel's decayed and abandoned dining hall.

I chose to make my visit to this hallowed ground towards the end of the summer of 1937. Having explained my purpose to the somewhat surly proprietor, I was eventually shown into the room that Horningtops had described. At the reception desk I had been informed that a sizeable number of musicians were in residence and I waited with some anticipation for them to come down from their rooms. After some time, it became clear that my wait was going to be a long one and so I took it upon myself to go upstairs to chivvy them along. The reception I received when I entered Bo Connoc's evil smelling habitation was enough to persuade me to delegate this task to my assistant.

Eventually, the one-time dining room filled with familiar, if not particularly friendly, faces in search of the free alcohol they had been promised. Endellion Trebetherick and One Arm Gunwalloe were the first to arrive, as ever arguing bitterly over some trifle; they were followed by Wheal Honey Brown, "Blue" Bob Polkerris, Cubert Washaway and the then still married Lil Gilmartin and Bos Coppa. Reginald Lanhydrock emerged towards the end of the evening.

As the session drew to a close, I recall looking around at the faded elegance of the smoke-filled room and at the straining and sweat-covered faces of the men and women who every year chose to return to this place when it was time to come in off the road. Candlelight threw flickering shadows on the walls, the floor beneath me vibrated with the muddy stamp of heavy boots, and the air filled with laughter and far-travelled melodies. I made a mental note to instruct Horningtops to keep his suggestions to himself in future.

Probus Strut

Date recorded: September 3rd, 1937

Performers: Kilhallon, Geevor; Kilhallon, Trethowel; Coppa, Bos; St John, Mabyn; Washaway, Cubert; Lanhydrock, Reginald; Nanstallon, Sonny Boy; Trebetherick, Endellion; Boswell, Ernest “Big”; Pelynt, Duloe; Amble, Chapel; Nancledra Towedrack; Unidentified, multiple.

Recordist: Valletort, Eric A.

Instruments: Fruitbox bass, copper string guitar, oil can guitar, ukulele, bass ukulele, concertina, soprano concertina, baling wire banjo, harmonica (low F probable), harmonica (high F), one row diatonic accordion, percussion (unidentified).

Setting: Secondary camp, Two Waters’ Foot.

Tape number: EAV1847

Track number: 9

Archive ID: on.soundcloud.com/s1npg

Technical note: Ambient sound, passing train (up Cornish Riviera probable), severe disc distortion.

Rights: Trad. arr Valletort

Notes on the session:

I have, on reflection, perhaps been somewhat uncharitable in my previous comments regarding the harmonica-playing twins Geevor and Trethowel Kilhallon. In my defence it should be pointed out that their musicianship was rudimentary at best (as evidenced by the recording here presented), and their understanding of social niceties was non-existent, but their story is one of some pathos and is perhaps worth telling.

One night in late 1924, the new-born twins were found on the church steps of Our Lady of the Wayside, Dunchideock by an inebriated Wheal Honey Brown who was on his way back to his room at the Lanteglos Highway Hotel after a night of revelry in East Taphouse. A kind-hearted and well-meaning soul notwithstanding his incipient dipsomania, Brown took pity on the screaming infants, picked them up and carried them, one beneath each arm, towards what he presumably considered safety. The children's mother, who had in fact merely put them down on the church steps for a moment while she went in search of cigarettes, soon noticed their disappearance and followed Brown's footsteps at some speed and with screamed threats of considerable volume.

Once the misunderstanding was cleared up, Wheal Honey Brown and the twins' mother soon found themselves in sympathy, and quickly discovered a shared passion for fortified wine. Within weeks they had set up home together in a small hut just outside Tredinnick and, despite Brown's regular absences and roadside adventures, for a period of time the family gave the appearance of some stability and even happiness. As the children grew, they would find Brown's discarded harmonicas lying around the abode, and from an early age both would attempt to replicate the sound they had heard their stepfather make. In his sober moments, Brown would demonstrate some of his techniques to his young disciples, although neither teacher nor pupils had sufficient patience for any real progress to be made.

This domestic idyll was shattered when the twins' mother, Kensa, died of tuberculosis in 1935. Wheal Honey Brown, despite his good intentions, soon turned out to be utterly incapable as a single parent, and the twins wasted little time in taking to the road. Though still barely in their teens, the pair soon learned to ride freight trains and soon developed a duelling harmonicas act which they took to the streets of Cornwall's market towns. From this endeavour they usually earned enough to feed themselves, but they were rarely welcomed anywhere for long, and neither twin was a stranger to the inside of penal institutions. Whatever misfortunes befell them, however, the twins' devotion to each other remained unquestioned; my notes remind me, for example, of the number of occasions when Geevor sustained serious injury while defending his sister's honour from the attentions of fellow travellers. Neither twin survived into their twenties.

Despite the considerable sympathy that the twins' plight engendered, I always made a point of ensuring that, for reasons of both musical quality and hygiene, their harmonicas were kept as far away from my microphones as possible.

Hangman's Lane

Date recorded: July 29th, 1934

Performers: Washaway, Cubert; Nanstallon, Sonny Boy; Sandplace, Trehan "Boom"; Trebetherick, Endellion; Pelynt, Duloe; St Cleer, Isaac; Nancledra, Towedrack; Horningtops, Perranzabaloe; Carluddon, "Crutches"; Boscarne, Blind; Treviscoe, Little; Unidentified, multiple.

Recordist: Valletort, Eric A (with unrequested assistance from Boswithick, Sir Richard).

Instruments: Concertina, bass concertina, soprano concertina, bucket bass viol, ukulele, bass ukulele, string guitar, banjo, harmonica (high F), one row diatonic accordion (Gunnislake Wet tuning).

Setting: Main exercise yard, Liskeard Gaol.

Tape number: EAV1853

Archive ID: https://on.soundcloud.com/1D3S9

Technical note: Ambient sound (penal), severe disc distortion.

Notes on the session:

Players of home-made or "improvised" instruments generally receive - in my view quite rightly - fairly short shrift from students of serious music. There is, however, a small but stubborn coterie within the fraternity of ethnomusicologists whose members, bizarrely, hold such musicians in inordinately high esteem. This esteem would appear to be based upon the mistaken belief that there is something inherently organic or genuine about a player whose instrument has been fashioned by their own hands from materials found in the immediate locality. An ardent adherent to this nonsensical theory was Sir Richard Boswithick, my former university acquaintance, amateur folklorist and governor of Liskeard Gaol throughout the 1930s.

I well remember his enthusiasm as, one warm afternoon in July 1934, he led me to the corner of the gaol's exercise yard where a group of men were attempting to make sense of *Pilmere* a Caradon worksong in 6/8 time. Amongst the bedraggled ensemble were several familiar recidivist faces, and a young man who stood at some distance from the rest of the group playing a species of one stringed bass fiddle that he had fashioned from a steel bucket, a fishing line and a broom handle. At the end of the song, Sir Richard called this young man over and introduced him as Trehan "Boom" Sandplace. He then demanded that the inmate give me an in-depth demonstration of his instrument in order to explain how it was made and how it was played. I feigned what little interest I could while Boswithick rhapsodised about the ingenuity and innate musicality of the young man before me. I believe that my semi-involuntary snorts would have amply conveyed the extent of my approval.

My assessment of the young delinquent's talent was confirmed when I started to record the men. It had been my hope to collect material of sufficient quality from this session to produce a long-playing record with extensive liner notes; as was so often the case on my travels however, these hopes were dashed instantly - in general by the ensemble's quality, and in particular by the infuriatingly insistent, arrhythmic dull thuds that emanated from Trehan Sandplace's bucket. The governor's decree that this bucket should be placed close to my microphone "as an example of indigenous convict musicianship" was perhaps the final indignity in what was a deeply frustrating afternoon.

My notes remind me that "Boom" Sandplace contrived to escape from Liskeard Gaol some months later having incapacitated several guards with a home-made meat mallet.

Back Road

Date recorded: August 31st, 1937

Performers: Porthkea, Shutta; Downderry, Narkurs; Tregantle, Slim; Rosenannon, Sticks; Trebetherick, Endellion; Gilmartin, "Pink" Lil; Portscatho, Solomon "Chips"; Gunwalloe, Arthur; Chatagnier, Bou; Gunwalloe, Arthur "One Arm"; Lanhydrock, Reginald; Johnson, Arwenack; Unidentified, multiple.

Recordist: Valletort, Eric A.

Instruments: Concertina (treble and bass), harmonica (C), harmonica (Low F), 9 stringed guitar, one row diatonic accordion, homemade zither, ukulele, banjo.

Setting: Temporary camp, Twelvetrees.

Tape number: EAV1876

Track number: 4

Archive ID: on.soundcloud.com/xm2Ru

Technical note: Disc distortion (severe).

Notes on the session:

Narkurs Downderry and Shutta Porthkea were unusual amongst the travelling folk of 1930's Cornwall in that their relationship was, by all accounts, both stable and monogamous. Naturally, romantic encounters between travelling men and women were not uncommon, but (as I believe I have made clear on several previous occasions) these encounters were in no way a fitting subject either for polite society or for my research. The tale of Downderry and Porthkea, however, was something of an exception, and is perhaps one worth telling.

The pair met whilst apple picking in Bedruthan in the late Spring of 1934. Narkurs Downderry was a former lobster fisherman who had fallen on hard times following a navigational mishap and the destruction of his boat; Shutta Porthkea, a pasty crimper by trade, had taken to the road in search of a more adventurous life than that to which she had become accustomed in Shortlanesend. It did not take long for romance between the two to blossom, and by all accounts they were inseparable all of that long, hot summer as they travelled from farm to farm, spending their days in the fields and their nights beneath the infinite stars.

With the coming of autumn, however, life became harder and, reluctantly, they made the decision to go their separate ways. They parted with the solemn promise to meet again at the Tregavethan crossroads at 12 noon on the first of March of the following year. Both were true to their word and after a winter of varying fortunes in far distant corners of the peninsula, they met in tearful joy at exactly the appointed time and place.

For many years, they repeated this arrangement - the harmony of their summers being followed by the sorrow of separation, a parting softened only by the certainty of their springtime reunion. Where they spent the winters remained something of a mystery, but during the warmer months, they were a common sight around the campfires, junctions and water towers of the Cornish Road; I myself remember coming across them and noting their humble good humour and quietly affectionate nature which stood in such stark contrast to the general boorishness of many of their travelling companions.

Then came the day, inevitable perhaps, but sad nonetheless, when Shutta Porthkea walked into the camp at Two Waters' Foot alone. In response to the questions that followed her, she told of waiting at the crossroads, first in hope, then in desperation, before finally accepting the bitter truth that Narkurs was not coming. What had happened to him, and whether his failure to appear was through accident or design, was, to my knowledge, never fully ascertained. What was certain was that he was never again seen around the camps and workplaces he had once known so well. Shutta Porthkea, now travelling alone, continued to follow the tracks and the harvests for many seasons until she too faded from view. (There was, however, many a tramp who in later years would attest to sighting her ageing form - always in springtime and always on the road towards Tregavethan).

The current recording comes from happier times, namely a warm August evening just outside Twelveheads in 1937. Of the many things that Narkurs Downderry and Shutta Porthkea shared between them, one was a single harmonica that they would take it turns to play. Their attempts to accompany the tune can be heard at various points throughout this session. As can readily be noted, neither could be described as a musician in any sense of the word. To their credit, however, (and in contrast to the inflated self-opinion of so many of their peers), neither ever claimed to be.

Bear the News Lowenna

Date recorded: May 5th, 1937

Performers: Tremar, Darite; Brown, Wheal Honey; Treviscoe, Little; Boswell, Ernest “Big”; Lanhydrock, Reginald; Unidentified, multiple.

Recordist: Valletort, Eric A.

Instruments: Concertina, bass concertina, ukulele, string bass, gravel shaker, harmonica, banjo, 10 button accordion, 2 stringed guitar, unspecified zither.

Setting: Main store room, Downdennick Sawmill.

Tape number: EAV1861

Track number: 3

Archive ID: on.soundcloud.com/7niSb

Technical note: Some severe disc distortion.

Notes on the session:

The Downdennick sawmill sat between a bend in the River Fowey and the single line that runs into Bodmin Road station. For many years the wood store at its southern end provided welcome shelter to men and women of the road during inclement weather. At the first sign of an incoming Atlantic storm, figures would appear from the surrounding woodland, and would quietly make their beds between huge piles of timber on the sawdusted floor beneath the mighty corrugated iron roof. The mill's owners habitually turned something of a blind eye to this practice, and tended, in fact, to show an unusual degree of understanding with regard to the vagabonds' plight.

When, however, the mill passed from father to son, the latter declared that no workshy layabout would ever again sleep under his roof, and that no foul-smelling vagrant would ever again feel safe on his land. To this end he contracted the services of one Pillaton Cleer, recently escaped from Liskeard Gaol. A former travelling man himself, Cleer was acquainted with many of said workshy layabouts, was aware of their movements, and was utterly assiduous in his efforts to ensure that none should again enter the dusty warmth of the woodshed. In this endeavour he was assisted by a homemade cosh and a large, slavering Alsatian called Cedric. Pillaton Cleer's effectiveness in his role was beyond dispute. Stories of his brutality quickly became legion, and it was a desperate tramp indeed who would attempt to impose upon the mill's hospitality.

One such desperate tramp was young Jack Tremail, who, having recently run away from home, found himself one storm-ravaged night lost and alone in the depths of the Glynn Valley. Trees swayed threateningly above him and the wind howled a ceaseless, ghostly whine. Many times he fell as he ran, desperate to find some semblance of a haven. Then, in the blaze of a lightning bolt, he made out the shape of the sawmill. Rejoicing, he made for its shadowy comfort and like so many before him, lay down to rest in the sawdust.

Tremail was found the next day drowned in the River Fowey. His head bore bruising from a blunt implement and his leg carried scars from an animal's bite. In his pocket was a letter to his parents promising to turn for home.

*

In 1936, following years of financial mismanagement and a serious fire (which may or may not have been caused by a vagabond's deliberately discarded cigarette), the Downdennick sawmill was closed down and left abandoned by its owners. Cleer and Cedric were unceremoniously dismissed, and once again took to the road where, according to my sources, they were, for the most part, treated with a remarkable degree of forbearance by their erstwhile prey.

The mill itself quickly returned to its former role as place of shelter for the homeless wanderers of the region. Free from the fear of a swinging cosh, men and women of the road once again found themselves drawn to the mill's grimy warmth, and once again made their beds amongst the relics of machinery and unsold mountains of timber. As was the case with other such ports of call, evenings in the sawmill would be spent in drinking, storytelling and attempts at music-making.

The recording of *Bear the News Lowenna* here presented took place on the night of 5th May 1937. A ferocious storm was blowing through the valley and, by the time of my arrival, the mill's storehouse was unusually full. A fire flickered in a darkened corner and around it sat a large number of men and women with a collection of battered instruments. My notes remind me that amongst the musicians were Darite Tremar, Wheal Honey Brown, Little Treviscoe, and, seated at a slight distance, struggling with a two-stringed guitar, Pillaton Cleer.

The session was not a long one. The storm raged outside, the music became louder and increasingly less bearable, and those around me became more intoxicated and ever more boorishly obnoxious. After an hour I could take no more, and so instructed Horningtops to pack up my equipment and guide me back to my car.

Further detail relevant to this recording may, however, be added as a result of a later conversation I had with Ezra Hatt, the disgraced former net mender who, one evening a few months later, eagerly appraised me of events that had taken place after my departure from the sawmill. In detail, he described the sounds he heard that night as he lay amongst the other tramps in the woodshed's hollow darkness: whispered voices, a muffled struggle, a rusted saw cranked into life, a piercing cry of agony, and then silence. In the morning, according to Hatt, few paid any attention to the empty outline in the sawdust where Pillaton Cleer had lain, to the small pile of his abandoned possessions, or to the glistening trail of blood that led from the mill to the banks of the River Fowey.

*

For the sake of completeness, I feel it should be pointed out that later sightings of Mr Cleer confirmed that, contrary to initial assumptions, he had in fact survived this unpleasant encounter. Witnesses, however, do agree that the man they saw begging alongside a flea-bitten and starving dog was no longer possessed of the required quantity of digits to be able to play even a two stringed guitar.

Lock 103

Date recorded: April 26th, 1937

Performers: Porkellis, "Blue" Bob; McLemore, Deviock; Boswell, Ernest "Big"; Connoc, Bo; Johnson, Arwennack; Trebetherick, Endellion; Brown, Wheal Honey; Constantine, Trevenan; Carluddon, Crutches; Lanhydrock, Reginald; Unidentified, multiple.

Recordist: Valletort, Eric A.

Instruments: Ukulele, bass ukulele, 2 string guitar, oil bucket bass, concertina, bass concertina, one row accordion (flattened VIIth), harmonica (high F), harmonica (C).

Setting: Dry goods store, Fowey Docks.

Tape number: EAV1834

Track number: 3

Archive ID: on.soundcloud.com/LPCUu

Technical note: Severe disc distortion, shipping movement, fog horn. Strategic fade out.

Rights: Trad. arr Valletort

Notes on the session:

Little is known about Arwenack Johnson, whose concertina can be heard at the beginning of this piece. He was a peripheral figure amongst the travelling musicians of depression era Cornwall, generally choosing to travel alone rather than in the large amorphous groups that were a common feature of the camps and meeting places of the time. Legend has it that, one winter's night, he had become separated from the woman he loved, a raven-haired Spanish maiden, whilst attempting to board a fast freight at Menheniot. Grief-stricken at this misfortune, he spent the subsequent years riding the rails of Cornwall in an unending search for his lost love. Unusually for a vagabond stricken in matters of the heart, he was not known for excessive drinking or violence, and he seems to have been held in a degree of respect by other tramps. His concertina playing could best be described as workmanlike.

This recording took place in the dry goods shed at Fowey Docks one foggy night at the end of April 1937. A group of travelling men and women had chosen to shelter in the building's warmth as they awaited the departure of the night china clay to Lostwithiel and points beyond. I introduced myself to those unfamiliar with my work and, after the usual alcoholic inducement, I was permitted to capture the group's music making on shellac. As well as Johnson, the ensemble featured concertina player "Blue Bob" Polkerris, his mentor Wheal Honey Brown, and Bo Connoc - the hot-headed young guitarist who had recently escaped from Liskeard Gaol (although I was of course unaware of this at the time).

A particularly noteworthy aspect of this recording is the "fading out" of the final verse. This was achieved by myself and my assistant slowly moving the recording equipment (placed on a goods barrow) away from the musicians as they played. This caused some confusion and consternation amongst them, (and ultimately led to threats of physical violence from young Connoc who took particular offence at my turning my back on him), but the overall effect was pleasing and had the further beneficial upshot of rendering inaudible Reginald Lanhydrock's disastrous attempts at improvisation on his homemade "windjammer" accordion.

Arwenack Johnson lived out his later years in a platelayers' hut at the end of the Coldrennick Viaduct. It is not known if he and his Spanish Lady were ever reunited.

Herodsfoot Jehova

Date recorded: 14th May, 1937

Performers: Tremar, Darite; Horningtops, Perranzabaloe; Porkellis, Blue Bob; Luckett, Slow Jack; Portwrinkle, Blazey; St Cleer, Minions, The Reverend; Unidentified, multiple.

Recordist: Valletort, Eric A.

Instruments: Concertina, bass concertina, ukulele, guitar, saw, harmonica, zither.

Setting: Street corner, North Cross, Burlawn.

Tape number: EAV1878

Track number: 5

Archive ID: on.soundcloud.com/Rbxx3

Technical note: Ambient sound. Disc distortion (severe).

Notes on the session:

The first time I heard the thunderous vocal tone of the Reverend Minions St Cleer was in the Menheniot goods shed one evening in May 1937. I had arrived in the hope of recording one-armed zither maestro Tudy Dunmere, but in this, as in so many other endeavours over my long career, I was to be disappointed. As I approached the shed, I could sense that something out of the ordinary was occurring within. None of the usual sounds associated with vagabonds' gathering places could be discerned – no clink of bottles, no shouted obscenities, no half-remembered songs, no fights erupting, and no unorthodox playing of kitchen utensils. Indeed, as my notes remind me, the only indicator that the shed was occupied was the unmistakable smell of damp humanity that wafted through its open door.

Intrigued, I peered inside. Around a central fire sat a number of travelling men and women. Their clothes were ripped and torn, their faces were filthy, and their eyes were fixed ahead of them to where, beside a small crane, stood the massive and imposing figure of the man I was later informed was St Cleer. Dressed in black, his hands clasped behind his back, an expression of utter ferocity stretched across his swarthy features, the Reverend returned the congregation's stares. He said nothing. His eyes followed me with contempt as I took my place at the back of the shed.

At last he moved. He raised himself to his full height and inhaled a huge echoing breath. He licked his lips. His words, when at last they emerged, were portentous, doom-laden and heavy with threat. In detail and through imagery of shocking intensity, he described the fate that awaited those who strayed away from the path of righteousness. The punishments he outlined were inventive, brutal and irredeemably eternal, while the opportunities for redemption he cited were paltry and laughably unattainable.

His audience shifted uneasily. Painfully aware that the path of righteousness was one they had abandoned long ago, the vagabond throng winced with each new threat, and cowered from the divine's impassioned gaze. The latter, once assured that those before him were under his spell, then, almost imperceptibly, began to offer the merest glint of salvation.

Perhaps not altogether unsurprisingly, this salvation did not involve penance, self-sacrifice or a return to rectitude, but rather a commitment to do the Lord's work by picking the pockets of those innocent congregants who might stop to listen to the Reverend's words when he took his message to the streets of Burlawn later that evening.

A number of those present, through fear for their eternal soul, agreed to this plan immediately; many more agreed when St Cleer and his assistants distributed several bottles of unusually acceptable whisky amongst them.

An hour later, I followed the ragged band into Burlawn. The Reverend marched ahead, his huge frame silhouetted in the moonlight, his motley disciples trailing behind. At last they reached a central crossroads where, beneath a street lamp, amongst the broken glass and sundry detritus of a Saturday night, St Cleer paused, threw his hat down onto the cobbles and bellowed the single phrase "Foulest of sinners!" into the night. Passersby, many themselves the worse for drink, froze and turned towards him. He fixed one and all with his terrible stare. He embarked upon his well-rehearsed discourse. Behind him ranged a number of musicians who, with varying degrees of competence, provided backing for his soaring verbiage and further diversion for the growing crowd.

This crowd, now transfixed, then became the feeding ground for St Cleer's disciples who moved among the rows of proto-parishioners and relieved them of any spare change or valuables that they might be too distracted to care for adequately.

I, of course, was appalled by the subterfuge I was witnessing. I was at the same time, however, quite impressed by St Cleer's dynamic range and so set up my recording equipment and attempted to capture some of what was heard that night. This led to an unpleasant moment at the end of the evening when, during the sharing out of the ill-gotten proceeds of the service - St Cleer received eight tenths of everything his vagabond band had accrued - the preacher required a similar contribution from myself. At the first hint of my righteous resistance, he demonstrated that despite his religious beliefs, he was not above resorting to very credible threats of very extreme violence.

I was not altogether surprised to learn a few months later that the Reverend St Cleer had been convicted of criminal deception and had been sentenced to eighteen months in Liskeard Gaol. Neither, in all honesty, was I shocked to discover that his bellowing had eventually, and permanently, been silenced one night by his long suffering cellmate, Sidney "Mainline" Feock, who declared that facing the hangman's noose was preferable to another day spent being metaphorically beaten about the head by the Reverend's sledgehammeresque sermonising.

Hey Bokiddick

Date recorded: July 29th, 1938

Performers: Lanhydrock, Reginald; Washaway, Cubert; Nanstallon, Sonny Boy; Trebetherick, Endellion; Pelynt, Duloe; Brown, Wheal Honey; St Cleer, Isaac; Nancledra, Towedrack; Horningtops, Perranzabuloe; Carluddon, "Crutches"; Boscarne, Blind; St John, Miss Mabyn; Unidentified, multiple.

Recordist: Valletort, Eric A

Instruments: Concertina, bass concertina, soprano concertina, bucket bass viol, ukulele, bass ukulele, gutstring guitar, harmonica (high F), one row diatonic accordion, spoons.

Setting: Temporary camp, Liskeard (Looe branch).

Tape number: EAV1832

Track number: 4

Archive ID: on.soundcloud.com/8D6xW

Technical note: Ambient sound, severe disc distortion.

Notes on the session:

Whilst waiting at Liskeard for the late-running Bristol Temple Meads on a summer's evening in 1938, my attention was drawn by the sound of distant spoons coming from a coppice along the tracks. I have written at length of my disapproval of improvised percussion instruments, particularly those which rely upon culinary implements; however, experience has taught me that such untutored rattling is often the precursor to more tuneful offerings, and it was with this in mind that I hurried back to the boot of my car to collect my recording equipment.

At the end of a rutted and dusty track between the main line and the steeply curving Looe branch, I came upon the source of the sound. Beneath a tree, beside a small flickering fire, sat Roscorla "Crutches" Carluddon humming to himself and attempting to execute some sort of syncopated accompaniment with the two rusted teaspoons he held between his gnarled forefingers. No other musicians were present. This left me in the most awkward of positions: Carluddon was clearly under the impression that I had come with the express purpose of recording his output (and immediately raised both the volume and tempo of his playing), while I, naturally enough, had not the slightest intention of wasting a cylinder on such meaningless dissonance. I was however fully aware of Carluddon's reputation for sensitivity to perceived slight, quickness to anger and propensity to resort to violence, and so made an elaborate show of setting up my equipment and preparing to capture his performance. Naturally I employed only blank cylinders for this apparent recording, with the consequence that two hours of tuneless singing and primitive percussion, interspersed with self-pitying anecdotes about a poverty-stricken upbringing in turn of the century Clay Country, were lost, quite properly, to posterity.

As night fell, we were at last joined by other travelling men and women. The majority had arrived on the eastbound Luxulyan, and amongst their number were Reginald Lanhydrock, Wheal Honey Brown and Blind Boscarne.

The piece here presented is the Taphouse standard *Hey Bokiddick*. As well as vagrant musicians' perennial inability to follow a basic tempo, the recording demonstrates Crutches Carluddon's infuriating stamina and refusal to bow to the common will. He was eventually silenced by a whispered threat of considerable severity from the usually unflappable Mabyn St John.

Fairline

Date recorded: September 3rd, 1937

Performers: Coppa, Bos; Washaway, Cubert; Lanhydrock, Reginald; Nanstallon, Sonny Boy; Trebetherick, Endellion; Nancledra Towedrack; Polruan, Arlo; Horningtops, Perranzabaloe; Carluddon, "Crutches"; Boscarne, Blind; St Cleer, Isaac; Treviscoe, Little; Unidentified, multiple.

Recordist: Valletort, Eric A.

Instruments: Copper string guitar, oil can guitar, ukulele, bass ukulele, fruitbox zither, concertina, concert concertina, soprano concertina, baling wire banjo, harmonica (low F probable), harmonica (high F), one row diatonic accordion (Cajun tuning).

Setting: Secondary camp, Two Waters' Foot.

Tape number: EAV1865

Archive ID: on.soundcloud.com/J1j3H

Technical note: Ambient sound, passing local goods train (late-running), severe disc distortion.

Notes on the session:

I came across harmonica player, vagabond and former sailor Arlo Polruan only once during the years of my research. This meeting took place towards the end of an evening at Two Waters' Foot (the recordings of which had been largely rendered unusable by the presence of Ezra Burlawn's notoriously discordant oil-can guitar) in the late summer of 1937.

Polruan was seated in a darkened corner at a small distance from the fire. I noted that he joined in with the music only sporadically, and spent much of the evening in silent contemplation, apparently oblivious to the raucous goings on around him. Somewhat intrigued, I took the opportunity of a break in the music-making (occasioned by a fight breaking out between the aforementioned Burlawn and Arthur "One Arm" Gunwalloe) to engage him in conversation.

Arlo Polruan was polite, but taciturn, seeming to have little wish to enter into small talk or discussion of our surroundings. When, however, I asked him about his days at sea, he waxed briefly lyrical - describing life on board, the joys and the hardships he faced, and the wonder of some of the destinations he had reached. Then, without prompting, he told me of his final voyage.

His tale may be summarised as follows: while on shore leave in Plymouth as a young matelot, he met and fell in love with a woman who worked in the Lyons Tearoom on Union Street. Her name was Miss Polly Millbay. As their mutual tenderness grew, the pair would meet each evening and would stroll the city's streets and waterfront dreaming of the day when the sailor could find work ashore and they might wed. From that time on, every time Arlo's ship left port, Polly would wave him off from Devil's Point; and every evening she would look out to sea and watch the sun dip below the empty southern horizon as she awaited his return. Each time his ship sailed into port she would be waiting for him at the foot of the gangplank. And each voyage he swore would be his last.

The call of the sea, however, was strong and Polly was condemned to many lonely months of awaiting the homecoming of her dark-eyed sailor. She became a familiar sight walking along the Dockyard wall or asking at the gate for news of her beloved's ship.

Finally, however, Arlo Polruan made good his promise and journeyed home for what was to be the last time. His discharge had been granted, and work ashore had been secured. In his pocket were letters from Polly expressing her longing for his return and describing her dreams of the life they were soon to share. And then, after months away, on a cold and foggy December night Arlo Polruan stood at the rail as the lights of Plymouth hove into view. The water was ice smooth and the sheets of mist muffled every sound. His ship slid past Devil's Point and into the dockyard. The ropes were thrown, the anchor was dropped, a fog horn rang out, and finally came the moment when, with his kit bag on his shoulder and with a skip in his step, Arlo Polruan danced at last down the walk ashore.

The mist cleared and he looked along the quay. Polly was not there waiting for him as she had waited for him so many times before. Arlo hurried away to their old haunts but found no sign of her. All night he wandered Plymouth's foggy streets, checking in every doorway and asking after her of anyone he saw. At last he was led to the Naval hospital where, in the tuberculosis ward, she lay dying.

I quote here directly from my notes: "Arlo stayed with Polly to the end, and held true to his promise of never returning to sea. Since that time he has wandered the roads of Cornwall searching for comfort that will never come. At night, I am told, he cries out the name of the girl who so patiently waited for him in the mist at the foot of the gangplank."

When Polruan had finished talking, he quietly cleared his throat and moved to the shadows beyond the fire. From the darkness came the ghostly sound of his lone harmonica.

(I would under normal circumstances end these notes with a comment about the paucity of Arlo Polruan's skill as a musician. Given the melancholy nature of his tale, however, and despite such a comment being fully justified, I shall on this occasion refrain.)

Spin Ye Matilda (Variation)

Date recorded: July 18th, 1938

Performers: Lanhydrock, Reginald; Boswell, Ernest “Big”; Pelynt, Duloe; Trispen, Ezra; Trelissick, Robert Washboard; Constantine, Trevenan; Brown, Wheal Honey; Tremar, Darite; Luckett, Slow Jack; Carluddon, Crutches; Gunwalloe, Arthur; Porkellis, “Blue” Bob; Treviscoe, Little; Unidentified, multiple.

Recordist: Valletort, Eric A.

Instruments: Ukulele, bass ukulele, guitar, homemade zither, baling wire banjo, concertina, bass concertina, soprano concertina, harmonica (low F probable), harmonica (B flat poss), one row diatonic accordion, violin (strummed), percussion (various unidentified).

Setting: South yard, Okel Tor Mine (disused).

Tape number: EAV1843

Archive ID: on.soundcloud.com/dtb39

Technical note: Ambient sound, severe disc distortion.

Notes on the session:

It was a warm and dusty summer afternoon in 1938. Slowly I made my way between the fallen branches that lay strewn across the path leading through the hillside woodland. Ahead of me, my sometime assistant Perranzabaloe

Horningtops sweated and grunted beneath the weight of my equipment as he climbed. I requested that he pipe down.

At last the gradient eased and we found ourselves in a clearing overlooking the valley. Below was the mighty sweep of the Tamar, and beyond were the interlocking folds of Devonian hillsides. Horningtops pointed ahead, and we followed the path towards the shape of a crumbling brick chimney reaching out of the trees. Excitedly, my assistant intimated that our journey was nearing its end.

Minutes later we stood amongst the ruins of the Okel Tor Mine. Surrounding the remains of the chimney were a number of squat stone buildings, all of which had lost the slate from their roofs and the glass from their windows; on the floor were abandoned tools and the rusted remains of machinery slowly being swallowed by the grass; and in the distance, resting in the engine house's shade, was a large, noisy vagabond throng. Tentatively, we picked our way through the debris towards them.

We were met, upon our approach, with the usual ignorance and aggressive body language that I had come to expect from men and women of the road. Many were clearly already inebriated, despite the early hour, and those that were not were apparently more interested in their card games and their revolting culinary manoeuvres than in welcoming a renowned ethnomusicological researcher to their camp.

Despite this unpromising start, however, I was not altogether disheartened, for I had noticed that among this collection of the waifs and strays of the Cornish Road were a number of characters whom, at a stretch, one might consider as having some stature, musically speaking (though, as I am always at pains to point out, everything is relative): Arthur "One Arm"

Gunwalloe sat beneath a rusted tin wagon extracting thunderous bass groans from the left side of his concertina; Ezra Trispen, once again on the road after his sojourn on Plymouth's Left Bank, strummed absently at his four stringed monster of a guitar; Bob "Washboard" Trelissick was showing anyone who would care to look the tattoo of Lenin that now graced his bethimbled fingers (courtesy of his cellmate at Liskeard Gaol); and, surrounded by a discarded tangle of pick axes, weeds and fuse wire, was the recumbent figure of Wheal Honey Brown, whisky bottle in one hand, harmonica in the other.

Seizing my opportunity, I seated myself amongst these denizens of the itinerant community and proposed that, instead of my recording their usual garish output, I should teach them a traditional Morris tune that, once learned, might be presented at Cecil Sharpe House as proof of the existence of a thriving pastoral folk dance tradition in the Cornish Badlands, and as evidence of my ethnomusicological expertise in unearthing it. Those around me looked somewhat nonplussed. In order to give them a sense of what I was after, I pulled out my descant recorder and played them an excerpt of *Spin Ye Matilda* (a merry little tune from the eighteenth century reputedly written by the Vicar of South Petherwin). When they had finished laughing, my audience eventually began, tentatively, to agree to my proposal on condition that I would share any profits made on the project. (I did not enlighten them with regard to the rigorously amateur nature of folk song and dance collection.)

I set up my equipment and, after a few run-throughs of the tune, began to record. It will perhaps come as little surprise to the reader that the musical ability amongst the ragged ensemble was insufficient to do any sort of justice to a tune of such delicacy and refined pastoralism, and that those around the fireside circle had, after a few abortive attempts at the Vicar's melodious air, soon reverted to the oafish groans, parps and clunks for which they were renowned. (To compound my disappointment, the recordings I made that afternoon were, despite my explicit requests to the contrary, given rhythmic accompaniment by a number of former miners from the locality. The hearing impairment caused to these men by years of working underground is, it hardly needs pointing out, flagrantly apparent in their playing.)

As the sun dipped below the trees on the valley's western hilltops, Horningtops and I made our way back through the arsenic-stained undergrowth to the wayside halt at Harewood. My head was ringing from the cacophony to which I had been exposed and from the shattering of yet another of my folkloric dreams. Upon my return home, wearied by the day's frustrations, I took strong drink and penned a letter to the Times railing against the decline in decency and moral standards in modern society. This letter remains unpublished.

Untitled 15

Date recorded: August 26th, 1935

Performers: Treviscoe, Little; Stepaside, Josiah “Tin Joe”; Lanhydrock, Reginald; Nanstallon, Sonny Boy; Pendinnick, Arnold; Pentecost, Cyril “Hambone”; Amble, Chapel; Nancledra Towedrack; Horningtops, Perranzabaloe; Carluddon, “Crutches”; Boscarne, Blind; Luckett, Jack “Slow”; Doublebois, Enric; Doublebois, Aleric; Unidentified, several.

Recordist: Valletort, Eric A.

Instruments: 4 string guitar, fruitbox guitar, ukulele, bass ukulele, melodeon, concertina, concert concertina, soprano concertina, bass concertina, banjo, harmonica (low F or B flat), one row diatonic accordion (Caradon tuning).

Setting: Goods shed, Latchley.

Tape number: EAV1872

Archive ID: on.soundcloud.com/fkLWC

Technical note: Ambient sound, disc distortion.

Notes on the session:

It was generally assumed that the desecration of Arnold Pendinnick’s grave was the result of a botched act of revenge by his one-time friend and long-term romantic rival Probus

Illogan. My research, however, has led me to an alternative explanation.

Pendinnick and Illogan met at some point during the summer of 1932 while both were eking out a living as peripatetic net-menders. Finding themselves in generalised sympathy with one another, and sharing a similar outlook with regard to the pointlessness of honest labour, the two took to the road and spent the next few years wandering the Duchy's byways and branchlines in search of the least inconvenient way of avoiding starvation. (This for the most part involved a mixture of casual labour, minor criminality and occasional forays into public performance based on Pendinnick's ability to play four notes on the left hand of a rusted melodeon he had found abandoned in a farm outbuilding).

This period of co-operation and camaraderie, however, was not destined to last. One evening in the early Autumn of 1934, as the pair built their camp in the woods just outside Breage, they were joined by a young woman named Carleen Trewennack who sat down by the fire and wasted no time in informing her hosts that she had recently run away from home and that she was in urgent need of both food and protection. With some alacrity, both men set about demonstrating their gallantry and suitability as companions and providers. Inevitably perhaps, these efforts soon developed a somewhat competitive edge and quickly led to friction between the men. As the trio travelled together towards the winter months, it was consequently of little surprise that the relationship between Pendinnick and Illogan progressed gradually from mutual mild irritation to profound dislike, before ultimately reaching a state of visceral loathing and murderous hatred.

Matters reached a head when Arnold Pendinnick, always the more proactive of the pair, took the opportunity of Illogan's sleeping off a night at the Rising Sun in Harrowbarrow to propose marriage to the fragrant Miss Trewannack. For obscure and unfathomable reasons of her own, and to the profound dismay and surprise of those that knew her, she accepted the offer and the pair hurried off to East Trevenan where they were wed in a brief ceremony led by the Reverend Simeon Sithney. When Probus Illogan awoke, it was immediately apparent that he was too late to take any preventative action, and he could only content himself with informing all and sundry of the vengeance he would exact when next he saw his former friend.

Perhaps unsurprisingly the relationship between Arnold and Carleen was not a long-lasting one. Despite his protestations of undying devotion, Pendinnick was at best an unreliable spouse and he had soon returned to his freewheeling, occasionally downright irresponsible, ways. After little more than a year, and upon the discovery that her husband had pawned her wedding ring in order to cover his gambling debts, La Trewannack left him.

Notwithstanding the apparent carelessness with which he approached marriage, Pendinnick was by all accounts devastated by this turn of events. For the want of any other recourse or occupation, he set out once more on the road, and had within a few short months drunk himself into an early grave in the paupers' section of the Shortlanesend churchyard.

It was to this grave that Probus Illogan (having been informed of the sad news) made his way a few weeks later. On a clear and moonless night, with gusto and a home-made shovel he set about his grim task and, after several hours' muddy work, had retrieved from the dead man's coat pocket the small piece of paper he came for.

I imagine it was of some considerable annoyance to Illogan when, a few days later, he was informed by the pawn broker to whom he presented this paper that the mud-stained ticket in his hand was long since expired and that the ring it pertained to had been sold to a passing yeoman. Similarly, one can only imagine Illogan's pique when he found out that Carleen Trewannack, far from being becalmed in spinsterhood and receptive to earnest proposals from former acquaintances, had long since moved on and was now happily living in sin with the sub-postmaster of Higher Condurrow.

Arnold Pendinnick's melodeon features briefly in this untitled recording.

Dawn on the Luxulyan

Date recorded: April 18th, 1936

Performers: Carharrick, Nancy; Boswell, Ernest "Big"; Tregorrick, Slocan; Lanhydrock, Reginald; Treviscoe, Little; Gunwalloe, Arthur (One Arm); Horningtops, Perranzabaloe; Connoc, Bo; Carluddon, Crutches; Porkellis, "Blue" Bob; Boscarne, Blind; Unidentified, multiple.

Recordist: Valletort, Eric A.

Instruments: Homemade maraca, ukulele, bass ukulele, 8 string box zither, 4 string guitar, zither, copper wire banjo, concertina, bass concertina, soprano concertina, descant concertina, harmonica (low F probable), harmonica (high F poss), one row diatonic accordion, guitar (open D tuning poss).

Setting: Dry goods wagon (third from rear), Luxulyan-bound freight. Vicinity of Tywardreath.

Tape number: EAV1854

Track number: 18

Archive ID: on.soundcloud.com/eaF4b

Technical note: Ambient wagon sound (internal), ambient railway noise, severe disc distortion. Snoring.

Rights: Trad. arr Valletort

Notes on the session:

As I stared out of the open door of the late running Luxulyan dry-goods, I tried to take comfort in the beauty of the scene before me. Dawn's first light was breaking between the horizon's distant folds, and one by one the rolling fields and farmsteads were washed with the sun's golden glow. Ahead, the single line climbed towards a gap between green hills filled by sky of the proudest blue, while beneath me, mist, thick and pristine, clung to the hollows and river valleys marking a silver pathway to the sea. At our approach, rabbits scurried away across white paths, kicking up small clouds of dust behind them before burying themselves deep in dry grass. Above the sound of the train's rattle and clang could be heard the dawn's chorus and the soft wind blowing the leaves in the trees and the crops in the summer fields. The smell was of freshness, dew, trainsmoke and hope.

Behind me however, the scene was less appealing. The wagon's murky interior was filled with vague, misshapen outlines of snoring vagabonds strewn among scattered piles of their meagre possessions; the air was thick with dust, stale tobacco and alcohol-laden breath. On the soot-encrusted floorboards, amid the remnants of previous cargos, lay empty bottles and musical instruments so battered they were hardly worthy of the name. Every man's coat was flea-bitten, every boot was holed, and every hat pulled down over every filthy face was black with grease and grime. Occasionally one of the men would cry out in his sleep above the wagon's roar - usually some pathetic plea to a long-lost lover - his voice would immediately be silenced by a sickeningly sharp jab to the ribs from a neighbour's elbow.

I had boarded this train the previous evening (on the advice of my sometime assistant Perranzabaloe Horningtops) in the hope of recording Stenalees Tregehan, the reclusive bandoneon player. Born in Nanpean in the early years of the century, Tregehan had for many years made a reasonable living dividing his time between playing for the congregation at St Edith's parish church in Lanreath, and for the paying customers at the Bright Star bordello in Menheniot. Painfully sensitive about the additional sixth finger on his right hand (despite the advantage this gave him when playing in the upper register), Tregehan hated to expose himself to the glare of daylight, and it was not coincidental that both places of work gave him ample shadow in which to lose himself as he played melodies both sanctified and lascivious on his wheezing monster of an instrument. When, however, his two employers at last found out about his alternative occupation (it is not clear who discovered what first, but, anecdotally, neither Reverend Arbuthnot nor "Pink" Lil Tredinnick were impressed by the revelation), Stenalees Tregehan's fate was sealed, both jobs were lost, and he soon found himself on the road with his outsized squeezebox on his back and nothing in his pockets except dust and eleven fingers. According to Horningtops, Tregehan had recently been seen in the Bodmin area and would likely continue his journey westwards on the Luxulyan.

It should come as no surprise that Horningtops's information was erroneous. Neither should it come as any great shock that the music I recorded in that wagon during the previous evening's revelries, before the whisky drinking and the fights became too overpowering, was of the usual boorishly low standard. I include a piece from early in the session so that the reader may judge for him or herself.

The sun cleared the horizon, and once more I looked out of the wagon's door. I stared down at the gold-streaked rails and tried to forget my frustrations, tried to take hope in this new dawn. One day, I told myself, my luck would change: my labours would no longer be in vain; my words would not fall on deaf ears; my subjects would not be talentless, tuneless oafs; my surroundings would not be grimy wagons and campfires, but green pastures, spring flowers and maypoles; the cannon of my work would garner admiration from my peers and grudging respect from my father; my offer to give the Christmas lecture at the DCFDSS would finally be accepted and my ethnomusicological theories would at last be acknowledged as definitive.

With the benefit of hindsight and decades of bitter experience, I believe that it is fair to say that I might have been saved considerable disappointment had I been a little more restrained in my expectations on that morning so long ago.

Appendix A - Complete Track Listing

1. Vale of Plenty
2. Trevithick
3. Wheal Honey Blues
4. Long Rock
5. Bourbriac
6. Portwrinkle
7. Penhale Was Yesterday
8. St Hilary's Hill
9. Shortlanesend
10. Pityme
11. Polhawn nights
12. The Girl from Rilla Mill
13. Alvina
14. Speak to Me of Menheniot
15. Unidentified
16. The Cross at Gwinnear
17. St Enoder's Tears
18. Ponsatooth Tuesday
19. Muchlarnick
20. Tregonna Steeple or Oh Tregantle
21. Venterden Belle
22. Kensa Blue
23. Delabole on My Mind
24. From Pillaton to Polborder
25. Up Polbathic
26. Kit Hill
27. Rose An Grouse
28. Arsenic Eyes
29. The Chacewater Lament
30. Manachan Quay
31. East of Godolphin Cross
32. Roll Me Stithians
33. The Dark Side of the Valley
34. St Macra's Moon
35. Trematon Yard
36. Gwannhenwyn
37. Down Line Menheniot
38. The Luxulyan Air
39. Lady of Lanreath
40. Nancegollan Road
41. Wheal Jenny
42. Sibblyback Strut
43. Stony Creek Moan
44. Tresillian Fields
45. Lady Relubbus
46. Chilsworthy Girl
47. I Knew Not
48. Cardinham to Lanivet

49. Lifton Rain
50. Higher Kelly
51. Probus Strut
52. Hangman's Lane
53. Back Road
54. Bear the News Lowenna
55. Lock 103
56. Herodsfoot Jehova
57. Hey Bokiddick
58. Fairline
59. Spin Ye Matilda (Variation)
60. Untitled 15
61. Dawn on the Luxulyan

Complete Field Recordings